Theater and Literature
in Russia 1900−1930

Acta Universitatis Stockholmiensis
Stockholm Studies in Russian Literature
19

Theater and Literature in Russia 1900–1930

A Collection of Essays

Edited by Lars Kleberg and Nils Åke Nilsson

Almqvist & Wiksell International
Stockholm 1984

Published with the support of grants from the Swedish Council for Research in the Humanities and the Social Sciences

ISBN 91-22-00668-0

Cover drawing by A.N. Benois

Printed in Sweden by
Graphic Systems AB, Göteborg 1984

Table of Contents

Introduction 7

Michel Aucouturier: Theatricality as a Category of
Early Twentieth-Century Russian Culture 9

Herta Schmid: Čechov's Drama and Stanislavskij's and
Mejerchol'd's Theories of Theater 23

Angela Martini: The Syncretism of Dramatic
Structure and the Failure of L.N. Andreev's Dramas 43

Lars Kleberg: Vjačeslav Ivanov and the Idea of Theater 57

J. Douglas Clayton: The Play-within-the-play as Metaphor
and Metatheater in Modern Russian Drama 71

Harold B. Segel: Russian Cabaret in a European Context:
Preliminary Considerations 83

Håkan Lövgren: Sergej Radlov's Electric Baton:
The "Futurization" of Russian Theater 101

Nils Åke Nilsson: Mandel'štam and the Moscow Art Theater ... 115

Introduction

In the first decades of the twentieth century, the period treated by the papers of the present volume, theatrical art broke free from both literature and demands that it perform a social and mimetic ("realistic") function. Theater became an art in its own right. Stanislavskij and the Moscow Art Theater lay the basis for this emancipation through establishing the supremacy of a single artistic will in the theater, that of the director. Stanislavskij's disciple Mejerchol'd and his followers went further, liberating theater from literature and compensating for the loss by developing *the art of the director* on all levels (adapting texts instead of "presenting" them, re-educating actors into acrobatic supermen, composing the production according to Wagnerian *Gesamtkunstwerk* principles).

Thus the great epoch of Russian theatrical art and experiment was full of contradictions. The victory of "theater as such", often proclaimed under the banner of the "popular" and "democratic", was in fact leading away from the traditional balance between the scenic and the dramatic which had been the *raison d'être* for theater as a popular art form since antiquity. The aim of this collection of essays is to discuss different aspects of this critical period, roughly corresponding to the years 1900−1930, in the development of dramatic theater in Russia, especially such aspects which have not been treated in the standard textbooks of recent years.

"Theatricalism" was a topical concept in Russian culture before and after the revolutions of 1917. Michel Aucouturier's contribution shows the expansion of "theatricalized" behaviour and "dramatized" biography in literature, especially Futurism, and the self-criticism soon evoked by the radical tendency to abolish the distinction between art and life. Lars Kleberg discusses the symbolist critic Vjačeslav Ivanov's utopian idea of the revival of theater on the basis of collectivism, another program that also implied the dissolution of theater as an art form.

Čechov, originally understood in the terms of the Moscow Art Theater's naturalism, was in fact full of theatricalism. Mejerchol'd, as Herta Schmid points out, was the first to show this in his production of

Čechov's farces in the 1930's. Leonid Andreev, after Čechov's death, wanted to become a playwright for both the Moscow Art Theater and the anti-naturalist stage, a venture which—as Angela Martini shows—was doomed to fail. A more fertile soil for new dramatic experiments than the big, director-dominated stages were the cabaret stages described by Harold B. Segel. Here too, theatricalism was paramount, but often the starting point was dramatic texts written by authors with a strong feeling for theatrical convention and devices like play-within-the play, whose Russian traditions are discussed by J. Douglas Clayton.

After the revolution, the lack of new dramatic texts with a political theme was striking. This gave the impulse for a new wave of productions where the director often became the sovereign *montageur,* using the text at will. Mejerchol'd's former assistant Sergej Radlov carried the work further, to the limit where theater almost surrendered, as Håkan Lövgren says, to the new mass art of the cinema. Voices critical of this development in the 1920's were raised from different quarters, and not only from the conservative defenders of "literary" theater. Nils Åke Nilsson discusses some little known articles by Osip Mandel'štam, pointing at the threat posed to theater by isolation from "the living word".

The eight essays of this volume were originally presented at a symposium organized by the Department of Slavic and Baltic languages in collaboration with the Department of Film and Drama and the Department of Literature at Stockholm University, April 21–22, 1982. It is the hope of the editors that the contribution will shed new light on some aspects of the dynamic and critical decades between the opening of the Moscow Art Theater and the establishing of a new—equally "literary" and "ideological"—Soviet theater in the 1930's.

Lars Kleberg   *Nils Åke Nilsson*

Michel Aucouturier

Theatricality as a Category of Early Twentieth-Century Russian Culture

I

The subject of this paper is not the theater as a sum of dramatical productions or a sphere of social and cultural life, but theatricality as defined by Evreinov[1], i.e. the specific function which is proper to these phenomena but which can also be fulfilled by phenomena belonging to other cultural spheres. My contention is that it is precisely the appropriation of this function as an aesthetic, and further as an ethical principle, which provides a key to the most characteristic features of Russian futurism and can partly explain its historical fate. My interest, therefore, will be not so much in the theater as in poetry. Considering that the clarification of this function and of its aesthetic significance belongs to the history of the Russian theater, however, I shall take the theater as a point of departure for my argument.

The first quarter of the 20th century was undeniably the golden age of the Russian theater. It is the period when the theater conquered a leading position in the cultural life of Russian society, as demonstrated by the fact that the most famous "modern" writers of the turn of the century, such as Čechov, Gorkij or Leonid Andreev, were popular chiefly as dramatists. On the other hand, it was also the period when the Russian theater, following the Russian novel, entered the international arena and became an active participant in and not only a passive reflection of the evolution of world theater.

Both of these facts are related to the activity of the Moscow Art Theater, whose triumph at the beginning of the century resulted from the meeting and mutual fertilization of Čechov's dramaturgy and Stanislavskij's stage art. The fruit of this symbiosis was that the aesthetics and poetics elaborated by Russian prose, especially the Russian novel in its most characteristic version as represented by Tolstoj (whose devices strongly influenced Čechov) were transferred

---

[1] Cf. *Evreinov, l'apôtre russe de la théatralité* (= *Revue des études slaves*, t. 53, No 1), Paris 1981.

to the stage. One of Tolstoj's most important achievements as a "craftsman of fiction" derives from his sense of the dependence of the meaning of any statement upon its actual context: hence the stressing of non-verbal communication, which modulates the signification of the character's speech and allows it to express all the levels of consciousness, including the deepest and the less verbalized. It is this feature of Tolstoj's art (which could be considered as the highest achievement of psychological realism in prose fiction), that Čechov, together with Stanislavskij, transferred to the stage, where the significant inner context (what was to be called *podtekst,* "the subtext"), on which the actual psychological meaning of the dialogue entirely depends, can be expressed by appropriate stage devices.

This belated transposition to the stage of the poetics of Russian realism explains the early twentieth-century Russian intelligentsia's almost religious devotion to the Moscow Art Theater. Stanislavskij's theater, like Tolstoj's novel, is devised and perceived by its public as the final suppression of artificiality, of any convention whatever: it is, as the critic puts it, a "paradoxical theater, which pretends to be not art, but life itself".[2] But in this striving towards "life itself", the dramatist (and the director) can go further than the novelist: reproducing life "in the flesh", i.e. in the medium of life itself, the theater appears as a privileged field for the ultimate execution of the aesthetics of realism. It represents the extreme limit of mimesis, which according to realism is the very purpose of art.

But the notion of a limit already implies the moment of negation. Therein lies the general significance of realistic theater for the history of Russian culture: it reveals the limits of realism in general, i.e. the internal contradiction of mimesis. Such is the point of Brjusov's article "The Unnecessary Truth": even on the stage, according to Brjusov, the suppression of convention can be only relative, since "the stage, by its very essence, is conventional / . . . / Not only theatrical art, but no other art can elude the conventionality of form and become a recreation of reality / . . . / Wherever there is art, there is convention".[3] Stanislavskij's celebrated "fourth wall" is deeply symbolical: it amounts to a suppression of the stage itself, as separated from and opposed to the audience, and thus points out to the limit

[2] F. Ferguson, *The Idea of a Theater,* New York 1955, p. 161.
[3] V. Brjusov, "Nenužnaja pravda", in *Sobranie sočinenij v semi tomach,* t. 6, M. 1975, p. 62–73.

which, if it could be reached, would transform realistic theater into a self-contained and unnecessary "reduplication of reality".

In contrast to the realistic theater vainly striving to "imitate nature" and to "recreate life", Brjusov extols the "consciously conventional theater", in which the only purpose of both the setting and the dramatist's text is to "supply all the conditions that will allow the actor's art to manifest itself as freely as possible and be perceived by the spectators as fully as possible". For, according to Brjusov, "in the theater, the aesthetic pleasure derives from the performance, not from the play". The artist, the creator, is not the dramatist, but the actor. "The author is a servant of the actors. Otherwise, the theater would lose its right to exist". Here Brjusov comes close to a definition of the specificity of theater as a thoroughly autonomous art that is not only independent of but also radically different from literature, since it falls into the category of the "performative" (or "artistic") arts, as opposed to the "permanent" (*prebyvajuščie*) ones, such as literature or painting.

But one cannot fail to notice that, Brjusov's accusation notwithstanding, Stanislavskij's psychological realism, with its stress on "subtext", leads to a similar notion of theater as a specific art whose bearer is not the dramatist but the actor. As a matter of fact, Stanislavskij's "system" is above all a method of training actors. The extreme realism of the setting, the decoration, the costumes, the accessories, the light-effects, are directed not so much towards the spectator as towards the actor: they are devised to make him experience (*pereživat'*) as real the situation which constitues the "subtext" and confers upon the text its actual meaning. Thus, the "subtext" which the actor must convey tends to prevail over the text itself.

Such an emphasis on the "subtext" can lead to a symbolistic reinterpretation of realistic theater, suggesting a second, incognizable level of reality. But it can also lead to Evreinov's "theatrical theater", where the dramatist's text is no more than a pretext for "transfiguration" which, according to Evreinov, is the "fundamental feature which distinguishes drama from lyric and epic"[4], i.e. the very essence of theatricality. The possibility of such a paradoxical metamorphosis of the realistic theater into its opposite seems to be implied by the

---

[4] R. Jakobson, "Petr Bogatyrev, expert in transfiguration", in L. Matejka and T. Winner (eds.), *Sound, sign and meaning,* Ann Arbor 1976, p. 30.

ambiguity of Stanislavskij's "fourth wall": devised as the imaginary recreation on the stage of the conditions of real life, if understood literally, it can only result in "theater for oneself", where author, actor and spectator merge into one person; and this, says Evreinov, is the purest expression of theatricality as an innate and therefore universal "instinct of transfiguration".

II

Thus one could say that the theater, by completing the development and bringing out the inner contradiction of realism, reveals its own essence as an aesthetic principle that is opposed to and replaces "imitation of nature". It seems to me that an illustration of this process can be found in Russian futurism.

In a paper entitled "Theatricality as viewed by Evreinov and the Russian Futurists"[5] Tamara Baikova-Poggi has studied the relations between the theoretician of theatricality and the Russian futurists. She notes certain facts which are accidental to the topic—for example their personal acquaintance and common political attitude—but she also correctly brings out the resemblance between the futurists' "word as such" (*slovo kak takovoe*) and Evreinov's "theater as such" (*teatr kak takovoj*).[6] No matter which of these mottos was first, and whether or not they appeared independently of one another, the point is that they represent the logical outcome of the same process by which art in general and its various forms became increasingly aware of what made them differentiated and specific. The specificity of poetry, that which distinguishes it from other functions of language, is "the word as such", that is, the word is not a neutral sign for a completed meaning, but a "thing", a solid material for the creation of a "verbal object". The specificity of theater, according to Evreinov, is theatricality, i.e. the innate instinct of transfiguration which impels us to transform ourselves into someone else. The purpose of acting is not the reproduction of a completed image, but the creation of a new

[5] T. Baikova-Poggi, "Teatral'nost' u Evreinova i u russkich futuristov", *Revue des études slaves* 1981, No 1, p. 47–58.

[6] *Slovo kak takovoe. O chudožestvennych proizvedenijach*, 1913; N. Evreinov, *Teatr kak takovoj*, SPb 1912.

being; not the duplication of existing reality, but the creation of a new, theatrical world.

The similarity of these principles is evident. Both of them derive from what Mandel'štam has phrased as follows: "When they speak to him (i.e. the artist) of reality, he only smiles bitterly, for he knows of the infinitely more convincing reality of art".[7] What is at stake here is the whole conception of the relations between art and reality. The work of art is no longer considered simply as an immaterial reflection of reality, but as a part of it, as a material object with properties of its own.

The limits of this parallel, however, are no less conspicuous. Advocating the "word as such" in his early, "futuristic" essay on Chlebnikov[8], Roman Jakobson defines poetry as "language in its aesthetic function". But he does not give any further definition of this function, only contrasting it to the communicative and the emotional ones: the "word as such" does not provide any aesthetic theory. By contrast, the "theater as such" is defined by Evreinov as the manifestation of an innate "theatrical instinct", considered as an attribute of life manifesting itself even in its lower, animal forms, and therefore even more fundamental than the aesthetic sense. It is clear that such an instinct, which is closely related to the instinct of playing, can be considered as one of the roots of art. It can therefore provide the "word as such" with the aesthetic foundation which it lacks.

Russian futurism seems to confirm such a conclusion. Attempts to reduce to a common denominator such a complex, unruly and theoretically confusing movement as Russian futurism usually lead to an emphasis on the "word as such" as its central tenet: "The history of Russian futurism", writes Vladimir Markov, "seems to me an imperfect and disorganized manifestation of a clear aesthetic idea, that of poetry growing directly from language."[9] A similar point of view is expressed by Krystyna Pomorska: "The main point in futurist aesthetics was the theory of the word from the aspect of the sound as the

[7] O. Mandel'štam, "Utro akmeizma", in Sobranie sočinenij, t. 2, New York 1966, p. 362.

[8] R. Jakobson, Novejšaja russkaja poèzija. Nabrosok pervyj, Praha 1921, p. 11; cf. Texte der russischen Formalisten, Bd. II, München 1972, p. 30.

[9] V. Markov, Russian Futurism. A History, Berkeley and Los Angeles 1968, p. 385.

only material and theme of poetry".[10] Such a definition reduces Russian futurism to cubo-futurism, the latter to the works of Chlebnikov and Kručenych, which in turn are reduced to the "autonomous word" (*samovitoe slovo*) and "transrational language" (*zaumnyj jazyk*). But it has been pointed out that poems written in "transrational language" represent but a meager proportion of Chlebnikov's and Kručenych's poetry, not to mention the poetical output of futurism as a whole. Judged by its own standards, Russian futurism then appears as a failure.

But this point of view ignores as secondary and accidental the features which in the eyes of the contemporaries constituted the essence of futurism, and which remain for the historian its most conspicuous aspect. Adopting in 1913 the label of "cubo-futurism", the Hylaea group actually joined a movement which had already achieved notoriety by some of the features it retained throughout all its existence. The manifesto became a symbolic equivalent of a gesture ("A Slap in the Face of Public Taste", "Go to Hell!") instead of a theoretical argument (as it still is, for instance, with the acmeists); gestures (manifestoes, public performances, extravagant behavior and clothing) became the principal form of communication with the "reader", who was now a spectator and a listener. Such features unify all the varieties of futurism and distinguish them from other poetic schools (such as acmeism), so that it seems difficult to consider them as just accidental and external. They all amount to the principle of theatricality, which transforms the poet into an actor performing the role he has himself invented before an audience. The poetic work itself becomes just a part of this role, and can be reduced to the minimum or even merely suggested: Majakovskij's public appearances and popularity with audiences anticipated his mature poetic production.

Only such a point of view can explain Majakovskij's recognized position as the leading figure of Russian futurism after Igor' Severjanin, whom he dethroned and who, up until the Revolution, remained his chief rival in the eyes of public opinion. The "word as such" has in his poetry an important but not autonomous signification: it expresses a deliberately "manual" attitude towards the arts

---

[10] K. Pomorska, *Russian Formalism and its Poetic Ambiance*, The Hague-Paris, 1968, p. 78.

and poetry in particular that considers the word as a "heavy, rough, visible" material.[11] This attitude is in its turn but one of the aspects of that permanent public demonstration of himself in the role of the poet which is the sole theme of his early poetry. In that sense, its novelty is altogether anticipated and summed up by the very title and subtitle of his first long work: *Vladimir Majakovskij. A Tragedy,* performed by himself in the Luna Park of Petersburg in December 1913. Here lyrical poetry becomes monodrama, which Evreinov defines as the leading genre of "theatrical" theater. This is also the case with *A Cloud in Trousers,* which was also at first presented as a "tragedy", and which, finally, is a "drama in four acts" rather than a "tetraptych". It exemplifies with classical perfection a new, "theatrical" form of lyricism that no longer consists in the imitation ("representation" or "expression") of an existing "inner self", but in a public and palpable self-realization in words through a dramatic succession of metaphorical transformations.

This new form of lyricism which is no longer contemplative or reflexive but active, "in performance", can be considered as the reflection in the sphere of lyricism of the futuristic aesthetics of the "transformation" instead of the "imitation" of reality. Its allegorical expression can be found in Pasternak's first prose work, written during his "futurist period", the novella *Apellesova čerta* ("The Mark of Apelles", 1915).[12] In this story, the Italian poet Relinquimini challenges his German rival Heinrich Heine to a poetic competition, the rules of which are suggested by a Greek legend (visiting his rival Zeuxis, the painter Apelles has drawn on the wall of his house one single line, by which he is to be recognized). As his "mark of Apelles", the Italian poet, known as the author of a poem on love entitled "Il Sangue", has sent to Heine the imprint of his bloodstained finger on a blank visiting-card: thus he proposes love as a theme for the competition. Heine's answer is unexpected: he finds out who Relinquimini's beloved is, and impersonating the lover, actually falls in love and makes her fall in love with him. Thus, to the traditional

<hr/>

[11] V. Majakovskij, "Vo ves' golos", in *Polnoe sobranie sočinenij,* t. 10, M. 1958, p. 281.
[12] B. Pasternak, "Il tratto di Apelle", in *Vremennik Znameni Truda,* M. 1918; cf. "Apellesova čerta", in *Rasskazy,* M. 1925; English translation in Pasternak, *Prose and poems,* ed. by S. Schimanski, London 1945, rev. ed. London 1959, p. 140.

lyrical poet who, albeit symbolically, "expresses" love, Pasternak opposes the poet-actor, who actually "performs" it.

When the heroine begins by calling him "a wandering buffoon" and accuses him of behaving as if he were on the stage, Heine replies: "We spend our whole lives on the stage and it is only with the greatest difficulty that some of us assume the naturalness which is bequeathed to us like the character of an actor on the day of our births".[13] The paradox of naturalness considered as a role is but the fundamental paradox of lyrical poetry which fuses two apparently incompatible qualities: artificiality as a necessary prerequisite of art, and sincerity as the specific "truth" of lyricism. The aesthetics of classicism, by stressing artfulness, seem to sacrifice sincerity; romanticism, on the other hand, by extolling artlessness, seems to forget about art. Futurism as represented by Pasternak (the whole novella may serve as a commentary on the poetry of Majakovskij) solves this dilemma by proposing the principle of theatricality as a new quality of lyricism, a new form of poetic expression of the self.

III

The sincerity of the poet-actor, both creator and performer of his own role, is not measured as in traditional lyrical poetry by the degree of resemblance between the poetic word and the inner world of the poet, but by the degree of self-oblivion, of absorption in the created role he can achieve. This, according to Pasternak's memoirs, is the feature that distinguishes Majakovskij from his literary surroundings: "As distinct from playing each game separately, he played them all at once; in contempt of acting a part, he played at life."[14]

Here theatricality appears not only as an aesthetic, but also as an ethical category. Such an extension is also characteristic of Russian futurism, and, deriving from its fundamental premises, partly explains its historical fate.

The celebrated claim of the cubo-futurists: "Throw Puškin, Tolstoj, Dostoevskij etc. from the steamer of contemporaneity", i.e. the

---

[13] *Ibid.* p. 138.
[14] B. Pasternak, *Ochrannaja gramota*; English translation in *Prose and poems*, London 1959, p. 96.

rejection of the art of the past, does not express an aesthetic choice. What they reject is not a definite style or taste, but all that *once was* and therefore *can no longer be* art. For art, according to their views, is a creative process, not a finished collection of things. In other words, the frontiers of specificity separate art from culture, which can be valuable as a testimony but has no aesthetic value of its own.

Hence the significance attached by the cubo-futurists to the "blots and vignettes of creative expectation", to spelling mistakes, to the original handwriting which they boast of reproducing in "books of self-writing (autographs), published by /them/ in Moscow."[15] Hence the striking motto "After reading, tear to pieces!". Here lies the authentic significance of "transrational language", which is not meant (as is often assumed) simply as a new language added to the existing ones, but as an absolute "language in the making", i.e. as the permanent unveiling of the creative process at work in language: it thus represents an implicit attempt to transfer poetry from the sphere of "permanent arts" (according to Brjusov's terminology) to that of the "performative" ones. This explains its relative rarity: it is an unachievable goal rather than a real program. For when printed, i.e. transformed into a fixed text, "transrational language" loses its deepest significance as language "in performance" or "in process". This is what Chlebnikov himself must acknowledge: "When being written, the transrational words of the dying Ekhnaton: *'manč, manč'*, in *Ka*, almost caused real pain; I could not read them for the lightning that flashed between the words and me; now they are nothing for me."[16]

Another striking feature of Russian futurism is related to the same opposition between art as a creative process and culture as a collection of finished objects (or mental habits): it is the paradoxical primitivism of poets whose literary label is an appeal to the future. Indeed, the nostalgia for a return to a primitive or precultural condition expresses a longing for living art, i.e. for art as a vital function (instead of just a cultural habit), as the immediate manifestation of a natural urge uninhibited by the conditions imposed by any finished and conventional genres, unlimited by the frames of any given material.

[15] *Sadok sudej 2*, SPb 1913; cf. *Manifesty i programmy russkich futuristov*, München 1972, p. 52.
[16] V. Chlebnikov, "Svojasi", in *Sobranie sočinenij*, t. II, München 1968, p. 9.

17

But it is evident that verbal creation ultimately cannot satisfy these implicit aspirations expressed in the futurist manifestoes for art as a natural, vital process. Only the theater, whose material is man as a whole, both his body and soul, whose productions are not dead objects but living performances, can wholly meet this demand. Herein lies the temptation and the danger of theatricality as the hidden aesthetic principle of futurism: it tends to obliterate the frontiers between art and life. This corresponds to one of the deepest aspirations of modern art as expressed by Russian futurism, but at the same time it conceals the danger of a theatricalization of life that is tantamount to its suppression.

Such a theatricalization of life is conspicuous in what Pasternak calls "the scenic conception of biography" shared by most of the poets of his generation, including himself, which he says he abandoned "before it bore any implication of heroism and before it smelled of blood".[17] As a matter of fact, the degree to which the self is implicated in an uncompromising performance of one's life as an invented role is illustrated by the similar fates of Majakovskij and Esenin, both of whom "heightened" rather than abandoned this conception, transforming their biographies into materials for their art (not in the sense of represented reality, but rather as a "transformed substance").

Yet not only the life of the individual, but also that of the entire society can be taken as materials for theatricalization, i.e. for art considered not as an imitation, but as a transformation of reality. Such an evolution can be observed in the case of the cubo-futurists, who accepted the Revolution in its most radical forms, with its dream of "transforming life", as a primarily aesthetic phenomenon. When Majakovskij writes "my revolution" in his autobiography, this statement must be understood literally: the cubo-futurists do not *join* the Bolshevik revolution, they appropriate it as a manifestation of futurist aesthetics. This explains their condescending attitude in 1917–1919 towards Bolshevism, which they considered as merely a lower, preliminary stage of the "third revolution, the revolution of the spirit."[18] The "Program statement of the communist-futurists", published in January 1919, reads: "Futurism is not just an artistic movement, it is an entire world-view which, while it is grounded on

[17] B. Pasternak, *Ochrannaja gramota*, quoted from *Prose and poems*, p. 111.
[18] *Gazeta futuristov*, M. 1918.

communism, in the final analysis leaves communism understood as culture far behind; futurism is a movement that deepens and broadens the cultural base of communism by introducing into it a new element—time—and the dynamism not of the masses, but of forms and time."[19] This "dynamism of forms, of time itself" seems to denote the conception of art as a vital process whose materials can only be life as a whole; this is what we have defined as an ethical extension of the principle of theatricality.

This theatricalization of social life is what the communist-futurists (*komfuty*) tried to realize during the first years of the Revolution on such occasions as the celebration of the first anniversary of October, when they transformed the whole center of Petrograd into a theatrical setting and when they directed "mass theatrical performances", the most celebrated of which, "The Capture of the Winter Palace", was directed by Evreinov himself in 1920. The basis for these attempts was formulated as early as March 1918 in the "Decree N° 1 on the Democratization of Art", published in the only issue of the "Futurists' Newspaper" (*Gazeta futuristov*): "The residence of art in the storehouses and barns of human genius—the palaces, the galleries, the parlors, libraries, theaters—is hereby terminated. In the name of the great march of the equality of all before culture let the Free Word of the creative personality be inscribed at the crossroads, on the walls of the houses, on the fences, the roofs, the streets of our cities and villages, on the backs of the automobiles, the carriages, and the streetcars, and on the clothing of all citizens. May pictures (colors) on the streets and in the squares bound from house to house in jewelled rainbows, delighting, ennobling the eye (taste) of the passer-by." Here, both poetry and painting lose their frontiers, becoming part of a general theatricalization of life.

This program developed into the concept of "the art of life-building" (*iskusstvo žiznestroenija*), one of the central tenets of the LEF. It amounts to the suppression of the "aesthetical gap" created by the bourgeoisie, who allegedly separated art from life. "The main task of the proletariat", argues Arvatov, "is to make art the creation not of forms existing apart from life (as easelpainting or chamber music), but of the forms of life itself. To create a joyful, beautiful life, and not

---

[19] "Programmnaja deklaracija kommunistov-futuristov", *Iskusstvo kommuny*, Petrograd 1919, No 8.

to 'reflect' it; to build, to fuse the artist with production, to unfold the richness of the human collectivity in real life, to design the material which makes people live in their everyday practice,—this is the truly lofty ideal which the working class deserves."[20] Or, according to Tret'jakov: "To colour (adorn) every productive movement of man with the skilfulness and the joy of art."[21]

Thus it is the whole social life of man which becomes the material for art as a transformation of reality. Art as a construction of life is opposed to everyday life (*byt*), which Tret'jakov defines as "a system of feelings and acts which have been automatized in their repetition", "a permanent order and character of the things by which man is surrounded"; this he contrasts to "existence, dialectically perceived reality in the process of uninterrupted creation." What he rejects under the label of "*byt*" is not just the automatized, usual, uncreative element in everyday life, but also everything that is instinctive, spontaneous, unorganized: "Every movement, every step people perform, their inability to coordinate themselves in their work, even to walk sensibly along the streets, to step into a tram, to walk out of an auditorium without pushing one another."[22] The aesthetic ideal expressed by this rejection of everyday life is that of a thoroughly conscious and organized collective life. "The beautiful is all that which bears the mark of man's organizing hand; the splendid is every product of human craft intended to overcome, subdue and master the elementary forces and inert matter." Thus, the ideal of a theatricalization of social life becomes the anti-utopia of the thoroughly organized ant-hill.

The final inference of this theory is ambiguous. The statements of the theoreticians of LEF can be interpreted either as a complete subjugation of art to the practical purpose of organizing social life (which brings us back to 19th-century utilitarianism), or as a total subjugation of social life to aesthetic criteria and values. But the complete suppression of the separation of life and art is fatal to them both.

In 1925 the critic and journalist Michail Levidov published an

---

[20] B. Arvatov, "Proletariat i sovremennye chudožestvennye napravlenija", in *Iskusstvo i klassy,* M. 1921, p. 87.
[21] S. Tret'jakov, "Otkuda i kuda?", *LEF* 1923, nr 1.
[22] *Ibid.*

apology of "left art" under the title "The Suicide of Literature?"[23] He thus expresses the internal logic of the principle of theatricality which, in my opinion, lies at the core of Russian futurism and predetermines its fate.

Pasternak symbolically expressed his rejection of the "scenic conception of biography" in his second work of short fiction, the novella "Letters from Tula", written in the year of the Revolution. The hero, a young futurist poet, is led by the sight of the theatrical behavior of cinema actors in everyday life to the disgusted rejection of his own past: "I am sick. This is an exhibition of the ideals of the age. The steam they are raising is mine, our common steam. This is the burning smell of ignorance and unhappy insolence. It is myself."[24] As a positive contrast to these actors there appears an old stage actor who has happened to watch the shooting of the film, which makes him feel as though he had been "thrown overboard from the steamship of modernity". But he finds peace as, returning to his lonely furnished rooms, he starts to repeat for himself one of his favorite old roles. "Theatricality" as an ethic of modern art is here condemned from the point of view of the traditional theater, an art which does not impose its laws upon life, but modestly performs its limited function. Thus, as one of the first to become aware of the significance of theatricality as a new conception of art and of its relations with reality, Pasternak seems to have understood very early the limits of this principle and the danger of its extension.

Paris

---

[23] M. Levidov, "Samoubijstvo literatury", in *Proletariat i literatura*, L. 1925.

[24] B. Pasternak, "Pis'ma iz Tuly", in *Šipovnik. Al'manach*, kn. 1, M. 1922; English translation in *Prose and poems*, p. 174.

Herta Schmid

Čechov's Drama and Stanislavskij's and Mejerchol'd's Theories of Acting

K. S. Stanislavskij and Vs. È. Mejerchol'd, the two most famous stage-directors in Russian theater history, founded two different schools of acting that used to be looked upon as mutually exclusive. Historically, one can state that both Stanislavskij and Mejerchol'd made efforts to adopt essential elements of the art of 'living through' (*preživanie*), as Stanislavskij's acting school was labeled, and of the art of 'representation' (*predstavlenie*), which was the label for Mejerchol'd's schooling method. Vachtangov, one of the most famous pupils of Stanislavskij, even tried to synthesize the two systems. Following Mejerchol'd's pupil Èjzenštejn, one can also say that *preživanie* and *predstavlenie* are two opposite poles between which the art of acting and staging in general oscillates, so that every theater system has to take both of them into account. Yet we must not overlook the fact that the hierarchy of elements constituting the theatrical system as a whole becomes fundamentally different if either *predstavlenie* or *preživanie* is given the rank of artistic dominant. Mejerchol'd and Stanislavskij were both well aware of this difference of hierarchy in their respective systems, so that their attempts of mutual approach were never driven too far.[1]

In their relationship to Čechov the playwright, both stage-directors behaved selectively. Stanislavskij, being a representative of the illusionistic theater, never staged Čechov's satirical one-act-plays, the so called vaudevilles,[2] and his performance of the *Cherry Orchard*, which work the author himself considered as a comedy, made it a tragedy, a treatment that evoked Čechov's vivid discontent. On the other hand, Mejerchol'd, who stands for the anti-illusionistic, so

---

[1] For the evaluation of both systems and their mutual systematic and historical relation, cf. Boris Alpers, "Sud'ba teatral'nych tečenij", in *idem, Teatral'nye očerki v dvuch tomach*, t. 2, Moskva 1977, p. 462–498. A slightly different position is held by V. Prokof'ev, *V sporach o Stanislavskom*, Moskva 1976.

[2] Except for the purpose of training, together with Sulleržickij at the MChAT II, cf. Alpers, "Tvorčeskij put' MChAT Vtorogo", *op. cit.*, p. 3–88, (39).

called conventional theater, never staged Čechov's serious major plays, except during his first years as a theater director. In 1935, however, he performed three of Čechov's satirical vaudevilles under the common title *Thirty-Three Fainting Fits* (*33 obmoroka*). The performance was supposed to initiate a new era of Čechov on the Soviet Russian stage; Mejerchol'd even thought of giving a special performance in Stanislavskij's apartment, because at that time the relationship between the former antipodes in the Russian theater world had become friendly on the artistic level as well as on the personal one, and since Stanislavskij was too ill to attend the public performance, Mejerchol'd wanted to come to him with the whole troupe. This intention, however, could not be fulfilled. *Thirty-Three Fainting Fits* was to be the last performance on the stage of the GOSTIM (Mejerchol'd State Theater) under Mejerchol'd's direction. During the last years of his artistic activity Mejerchol'd also cherished the dream of staging the *Cherry Orchard*. This dream could not be fulfilled, either. Mejerchol'd's preference for the *Cherry Orchard* was by no means incidental. One can say that Mejerchol'd discovered the comical, even satirical Čechov, and in doing so he statisfied two needs of his time, one being the need of making Čechov acceptable again on the Soviet Russian stage after long years of discrimination, which was only possible through the socially critical elements in Čechov's plays, the other being a new approach to the satirical genre in general and to the theatrical satire in particular. Soviet cultural policy disapproved of non-affirmative artistic utterances, and its guardians reacted especially sensitively to criticism in the theater. The genre of comedy in general, therefore, although it was deeply rooted in the Russian satirical tradition, had declined in Soviet Russia, and modern satirical writers had suffered persecution. Laughter eventually disappeared from the Soviet stage, and only the classical comedies were staged any longer. This created a gap in the theater repertoire, and Mejerchol'd's rediscovery of the comical Čechov can be considered as a contribution to the resurrection of a dying genre.[3] On the other hand, Stanislavskij's predilection for the tragical Čechov did little to make Čechov acceptable in the new society that demanded positive, optimistic heroes instead of the whining weaklings Čechov's heroes were considered to be. Thus, in

[3] Cf. Alpers, "Žanr sovetskoj komedii", *op. cit.*, p. 185–190.

the 20s and 30s, Čechov's drama was almost forgotten, so that Mejerchol'd's attempt in 1935 was indeed a contribution to the beginning of a new era in the aesthetical reception of Čechov.

The relationship of either of the stage directors to Čechov, however, cannot be properly evaluated if only the external cultural and political situation in Soviet Russia is taken into account. There also exists an inner connection between Stanislavskij's theatrical illusionism and the tragical aspects in Čechov's plays on the one hand, and between Mejerchol'd's anti-illusionistic, antimimetic conventional theater and the comical Čechov on the other hand. There is a hint of this relationship in G. E. Lessing's remark that the effect of compassion intended by the tragedy needs illusion, whereas the effect of laughter intended by the comedy tolerates distance.[4] When we describe the essence of *pereživanie* and *predstavlenie* in more detail below, we shall enter more deeply into a discussion of this connection.

The Moscow Art Theater (MChAT), managed by Stanislavskij and Nemirovič-Dančenko was considered as *the* Čechov theater, because its performance had secured the author's reputation as a serious playwright; his funny vaudevilles had been accepted long before the big plays and enjoyed lasting success. The technique of *pereživanie* taught at Stanislavskij's school of acting sought to awaken the inner creativity of the MChAT actors in order to establish a true relationship between the inner world of the actor as an individual and the external dramatic role which he was going to present on the stage. The technique of *pereživanie*, therefore, did not really blur the knowledge of the difference between the actor and his role, either for the actor himself or for the spectator, but the actor had to bring his inner life into the role, and the elements of his inner life had to be true ones: under the given circumstances of the role, the illusionistic nature of which could not be forgotten, the unfolding of emotions, moods and their corresponding outer expressions had to be 'real'.[5] Thus Stanislavskij introduced the art of psychological acting on the stage; he consequently used 'realistic' everyday settings and 'real' things on the stage to help the actors to establish true relationships to them. This

---

[4] G. E. Lessing, Hamburg, *Hamburgische Dramaturgie*, 42. Stück.
[5] Cf. K. S. Stanislavskij, *Sobranie sočinenij v vos'mi tomach*, t. 2 (*Rabota aktera nad soboj*), Moskva 1955.

psychological and everyday realism corresponded to the psychological motivation of Čechov's 'everyday drama' (*bytovaja drama*) and to the realistic current in Russian 19th-century literature in general. Stanislavskij's predilection for Čechov's serious, psychological dramas is therefore organic and self-evident. But what about Mejerchol'd's liking for the comical, satirical Čechovian drama? As to the vaudevilles, we need not especially stress that they demand a non-psychological treatment, given the traditional rank of the genre in Russia; the Mejerchol'd stagings of the vaudevilles, however, were intended to begin an era of re-evaluation of Čechov's entire dramatic production, so that the satirical element also seems to be present in the major plays, although Stanislavskij's interpretation did not permit it to come to the fore.

The concept of satire always includes a distance between the author and the fictional character out of which a cool, negative judgement towards the character is either formulated in the text or suggested. The concept of satire is also connected with realism: the negative fictional character (or his social surroundings) are supposed to correspond to non-fictional reality, although the correspondence is not a simple mimetic one – the fictional world usually exaggerates and distorts the real world.

Where are these two elements of satire in Čechov's major dramas to be found? I find them in three of Čechov's typical dramatic devices.

1. On the level of the dramatic characters, Čechov has a tendency to treat the minor characters of the plays in the manner of the caricaturist. Such caricatures are, for example, the teacher Medvedenko, Maša's later husband, in *The Seagull* and the teacher Kulygin, Maša's husband, in *The Three Sisters*, or "the horse" Simeonov-Piščik in *The Cherry Orchard*. The caricaturistic view is not always so evident as in these cases; thus Marina, the kind, fat nurse in *Uncle Vanja*, can also be considered as a caricature if one follows closely the author's intention with this character.[6] Comical characters on the level of the minor characters are common in the history of the comedy, but in Čechov's plays they fulfill a special function: they

---

[6] Cf. Herta Schmid, "Der Aufbau der thematischen Bedeutung in Ostrovskijs 'Groza' (Das Gewitter) und Čechovs 'Djadja Vanja' (Onkel Vanja), in: A.G.F. van Holk (ed.), *Zugänge zu Ostrovskij—Approaches to Ostrovskij*, Publications of the Slavic Institute of the University of Groningen, vol. 1, Bremen 1979, p. 3–89.

share one or two characteristic features with the serious main characters, but lack the psychological complexity of the latter. They therefore function as a mirror for the main characters, reflecting them in an exaggerated and distorted manner. Čechov used the technique of the "magnifying glass" (*uveličivajuščee steklo*) long before Majakovskij. He does it with a critical, satirical purpose. Thus, for exampel, the narrow-minded and both physically and mentally static nurse Marina symbolizes the social surroundings that suffocate the creativity in Uncle Vanja and Astrov, who, because they surrender so easily to the obstacles in life, are thereby unmasked as incarnations of the intellectual 'weaklings' of Čechov's time. By reflecting the complex, often sympathetic main characters in the distorting mirror of the secondary ones, Čechov utimately seeks to criticize a really existing human type, the so called neurasthenical type of the 90s in Russia.

2. On the level of dramatic roles and behavior, the Czechoslovakian stage director and theoretician of the theater Jindřich Honzl has made a surprising observation. At the end of *Ivanov* (IV, 10), Čechov's first published major drama, the main character discovers his identity with Pierrot, a melancholic standard character of the *commedia dell'arte*.[7] The standard characters are created by the history of theater. They consist of an unalterable set of signs like the mask, the costume, stereotyped expressions, and ways of behavior and acting. Before the revolutionary work of Stanislavskij, the normal actor would specialize on one standard character and reproduce, say, the young hero and lover, as long as he was physically able. Stanislavskij, then, destroyed the standard characters, but before him Čechov the playwright made them seemingly superfluous by the individualizing psychological treatment that he gave to each of his characters. While traditional drama would introduce the scheme of the stereotyped character to which the role of the play corresponded right from the beginning of the play, so that the spectator knew at once what he could expect from each of the dramatic heroes, Čechov's Ivanov starts his dramatic life with a search for his individuality. It is not until the end that he discovers together with the spectator that he was merely playing a standard role. The discovery of the traditional scheme behind the mask of the individual does not

[7] Cf. Jindřich Honzl, "Herecka postava", in: *idem, K novému významu umění*, Praha 1956, p. 239–245.

always constitute a life drama, as in *Ivanov*. But stereotyped characters or aspects of them are to be found everywhere in the major plays. Thus in *The Seagull*, Arkadina represents indeed the traditional dramatic *emploi* and its technique: confronted with Maša, whose unhappiness makes her lazy and weary, Arkadina reveals the physical discipline that has protected the beauty of her body from age and enables her to play the *Lady with the Camelias*, although she is over forty. This indicates that Arkadina is based on the stereotype of the young female lover, but unlike Ivanov in Čechov's first play, who commits suicide after his discovery, she is proud of herself. In *Uncle Vanja*, we find in the doctor Astrov features of the cynical raisonneur, and at the same time he reminds us of the lucky clown of the traditional clown pair; the other, unlucky clown is incarnated by Vanja: with regard to Elena, his beloved, Vanja is honest and without luck, while Astrov, who agrees to cheat Elena's husband in an "episode", wins Elena's favor. The same triangular constellation of characters and roles is found in Blok's *Balagančik*, where the traditional prototypes of the clown pair, Pierrot and Harlequin, compete for Colombine. In *The Cherry Orchard*, we again meet with this clown triangle in Epichodov, Jaša and Dunjaša. In *The Three Sisters*, Čechov uses the technique of tell-tale names, a device that is analogous to the stereotyped characters; the name foretells the dramatic fate of the character like the mask and the costume and the traditional name with respect to the stereotype. Thus Veršinin has the nickname "the lovesick major" (*vljublennyj major*), which has associations with the Don Juan-tradition and foretells Veršinin's and Maša's fate in the play. Analogously, to those who are familiar with the negative semantic values that Čechov usually attributes to the concept of love, the first name of the heroine in *The Cherry Orchard*, Ljubov' Andreevna Ranevskaja, foretells the unhappy influence of her romantic feelings on her dramatic actions; here, once again, Epichodov's nickname "22 misfortunes" (*22 nesčast'ja*) emphasizes by amplification the negative value of the love theme on the level of the minor characters.

While his handling of the secondary characters throws a critical light on the main characters and through them on non-fictional reality, Čechov's treatment of the stereotyped dramatic roles unmasks the inability of his complex psychologic characters to become autonomous personalities and is thus suitable for reducing the total psychological motivation of the dramatic characters as a whole. Although each character claims to be an individual personality and therefore has to be understood as fully responsible for all his utterances and behavior, Čechov at the same time shows that such claims are unjustified; consequently, he reduces the character's responsibility for himself. One of the most effective ways in which Čechov attains his goal of establishing an inner view of the character (created by the character's claim to be an autonomous individual) and an outer view (from which the reduced autonomy becomes visible) is simultaneously to be found on the level of dialogue.

3. On this level we find a phenomenon that I propose to call textual montage. Textual montage produces the well known effect of being at cross-purposes in dialogue (*Aneinandervorbeireden*): the utterance of one speaker, whether or not it is addressed to a partner in the speech-situation, is followed by the second speaker's nonsensical reply. The absurdity of this reply may have various explanations (the second speaker either does not listen to the first, or he purposely ignores his utterance, or he catches only part of its meaning). The superficial effect of the nonsensical dialogue is usually comical, but there is often a second meaning beneath the surface. Since none of the speakers is aware of this meaning, it is the author[8] who creates it by using the speaker's utterance as combinatory elements in an 'utterance' of his own. Čechov uses textual montage for different purposes. In *The Three Sisters* (I) the initial dialogue between Ol'ga and Irina is crossed with lines from the scenic background, where Tuzenbach and Solenyj are engaged in a game. The synthetic effect of the crossing here is an ironical author's comment (conveyed through Tuzenbach's and Solenyj's utterances) on Irina's and Ol'ga's dreams of Moscow and a better future that foretells the fruitlessness of these dreams. In the conversation between Andrej and Ferapont (III) in the same play, Ferapont's utterances, which are intended as replies to Andrej's confession, lack the inner connection with Andrej's lines, because Ferapont, due to his deafness, misses the exact meaning of what Andrej says. The final result of the textual montage here is a very subtle author's comment on Andrej's social position; Andrej talks about his private misfortune and does not listen to what Fera-

---

[8] Here and below the 'author' is always to be understood as inherent to the textual structure. He is never identical with Čechov as an individual.

pont says, while Ferapont mentions examples of social disorder. Thus here the author is hinting at the asocial behavior of the intellectual class to which Andrej Prozorov belongs.[9] While in the last example it is the physical defect of one speaker that makes it possible for the author to insert his comment in an otherwise dialogical situation, in Čechov's plays it is normally the device of the polyphonic construction of the character's utterances, conditioned by the assemblage of several (more than two) equally entitled speakers in the same speech situation, that provides the background for the textual montage. Thereby it becomes a potentially omnipresent device that allows the author to reduce the psychological motivation of the text and to introduce an artistic and artificial motivation of it that corresponds to the reduction of psychological insight into the dramatic characters and their roles.

Beside textual montage there is another device through which the author comments on his dramatic characters, namely the use of scenic props, which Čechov brings into a visible or audible connection with his dramatic characters. In *The Cherry Orchard*, where this device is particularly frequent it is even condensed in the minor figure Epichodov, whose nickname "22 misfortunes" characterizes not only his romantic relationship to Dunjaša, but also his relationship to scenic objects: Epichodov constantly fights against things (his new boots, a vase, billiard cues, a hat-box, and so on) and looses this fight, underlining by his exaggerated awkwardness the general falseness between men and objects in this play (above all the 'false' relation between the owners and the cherry orchard). In *The Three Sisters,* the falsehood of the man-object-relation is brought to the fore in the presents Irina receives on her birthday, and here as in *The Cherry Orchard* the small scenic attributes hint at the falseness of the whole life-situation of the dramatic heroes—the three sisters are unable to protect their house and family—(their brother Andrej, who incarnates their hopes of going back to Moscow) against intruders (Nataša and Protopopov) and parasites (Čebutykin, who does not pay the rent). In *Uncle Vanja,* the way in which props function as vehicles for authorial comment becomes evident in the stage direction referring to the map

---

[9] Ferapont tells of a merchant who overate and of a cord that is said to be tied through Moscow. The absurdity of these stories reveals a lack of social consciousness and responsibility for which the intellectual class, normally the educator of a society, has to be made responsible.

of Africa hanging on the wall (IV), as it stresses the uselessness and thereby senselessness of the map for the characters.[10] In this early play, Čechov uses the voice of the dramatic author to verbalize the general meaning of the man-object-relation in his plays; in the later works this relation is only suggested.

Summarizing thus far, we can state that the satirical element is constructed in the plays in the following manner: Čechov constructs dramatic characters who are too weak to fulfill their own claim of becoming autonomous individuals. These psychologically constructed characters are mirrored in the non-psychological minor characters in an openly ironical way, the ultimate intentional object of this irony being not the fictional dramatic characters, but the non-fictional counterparts which they represent, namely the neurasthenic intellectuals of Čechov's time. The mirror relation between main and secondary characters creates a distance from where the spectators look upon the main characters and laugh at them. At the same time, the scheme of standard roles which, since it is necessary for the representation of the main characters, overshadows the psychological, individualizing manner of acting, demands that the actors create an inner distance to their roles. This enables them to make clear for the spectator that the characters they are going to represent, voluntarily or involuntarily, fall back into traditional theatrical patterns. The effect of this discrepancy between claim and fulfillment on the spectator will be laughter and irony. With regard to the non-fictional counterparts of the dramatic characters, this irony will assume the form of critical and self-critical observation of human behaviour and its social conditions. And, last but not least, the device of authorial comment expressed by textual montage and 'speaking things' creates within the textual structure of the plays a subjective viewpoint for the dramatic author from which his attitude toward the characters and their claims for full autonomy becomes evident.

The summary of the satirical devices also shows that satire in Čechov's plays presupposes psychological insight into the inner life of the characters and their psychologically motivated acting, since it is the failure of the characters to become integral psychological personalities that ultimately evokes the laughter of the spectator. Thus Čechov's plays offer the spectator the difficult task of looking at the

---

[10] "Na stene karta Afriki, vidimo nikomu zdes' ne nužnaja."

dramatic characters from the inside, of suffering with them, as in the tragedy, and of observing them from the outside and laughing at them, as in the comedy. Finally and at the same time, they give him the opportunity to observe and laugh at himself, insofar as his life resembles that of the character.

The roles (at least the main roles, the minor characters being generally flatter) have to be acted in a double way: on the one hand, the characters' claims that they are autonomous has to be taken seriously, which means that the method of acting will be that of psychological *pereživanie*. On the other hand, the failure of the claim can only be expressed by the technique of *predstavlenie*, because only this way of acting allows the actor to stay outside the dramatic character and to express by non-psychological means the ironical and critical view contained in the author's comments. As a result one can say that Stanislavskij and Mejerchol'd were both right and wrong in their way of treating Čechov. Stanislavskij did justice to the dramatic characters' efforts to become individuals; then, due to the tragical genre, their failure had to be lived through inside the characters as a life tragedy. Mejerchol'd followed the outer viewpoint from which the dramatic author exposes his characters to irony and laughter. Neither of them saw that the tragedy of the dramatic characters becomes a satire and that the satire presupposes the tragedy. Thus both stage directors deleted something from Čechov's plays that constitutes their paradox and their aesthetic value. These were not arbitrary cuts, but resulted from the directors' artistic systems.

Stanislavskij's concept of acting can be described as containing a negative and a positive aspect. The negative aspect is included in the director's destructive attitude to the history of the art of acting: he opposed the traditional manner of acting that was connected with the conventional stereotyped roles. By destroying the traditional role-patterns, Stanislavskij also destroyed the theretofore usual specialization of the actors. He wanted every actor to be able to perform a wide variety of dramatic roles. The traditional role patterns are described by a stable set of signs, and are taken from the socially conventionalized and therefore mechanical mimical signs that belong to human communication in general. In order to become artistic signs (as constituents of theatrical role patterns) these social signs undergo a process of intensification or weakening, of selection and combination according to aesthetical laws. The actor would learn to reproduce the set of signs of just one traditional role pattern and make it shine through all the individual heroes he represented in his artistic life, so that the audience, once it had become familiar with the role pattern of a particular actor, could expect it whenever he played. The main task of the actor was to bring his one role pattern to perfection by means of endless repetition and variation, in which process the automatic 'memory' of his muscles was the most important factor. In his struggle against these traditional role patterns, Stanislavskij aimed at enthroning a new type of artistic signs within the sign repertoire of the actors—and this constitutes the positive aspect of his concept of acting. The new type of signs was taken from the spontaneous, non-conventional signs that every human individual inherently has at his disposal. The main means of expression are the eyes and the voice,[11] so that both of these became most important for the new type of actor; but ultimately Stanislavskij intended to create an art of acting that would subordinate the whole body of the actor and even his relation to the scenic surroundings to spontaneous expression. By means of spontaneous expressive signs Stanislavskij wanted to destroy the theatrical "lie" which he saw in the fact that the traditional actor evoked emotions in the spectator without sharing these emotions. He wished to re-establish truth in the theater by insisting that the actor first evoke emotions within himself, express them by individual non-conventionalized signs and, through these signs, make the spectator share his true emotions toward the dramatic character represented by the actor. But apart from the struggle for truth in the theater that is a part of the realistic current in Russian art, Stanislavskij's system can be described as an attempt to enrich the repertoire of theatrical signs through a new, non-conventional kind of signs founded on true emotions, and as an attempt to reorganize the whole system of theatrical signs by giving the expression of the face, above all the eyes, and the voice the position of the dominant, thus destroying the old dominance of the stable mimic mask such as it had been established by the traditional role patterns.

Stanislavskij's innovation in the field of acting had three consequences for the actors. First, they had to forget their usual devices of performing; second, they had to learn the technique of living through

[11] Cf. Lessing, 1. Stück. Cf. also Jindřich Honzl, "Mimický znak a mimický priznak", in idem, Zaklady a praxe moderneho divadla, Praha 1963, p. 25–43.

their role on the stage and of giving expression to their inner sensations by individually and spontaneously discovered signs expressed by their faces, voices, and bodies; third, they had to mobilize all their imaginative and emotional capacities in order to learn how to live through not just one dramatic character, but all possible ones, since specialization was no longer allowed.

In the discussions of Stanislavskij's concept of the new art of acting many objections have been formulated regarding the effects of the so called psychotechnique of acting on the physical and psychic health of the actors. One interesting remark by Jindřich Honzl on the consequences for the system of theatrical signs should be mentioned here. According to Honzl, Stanislavskij impoverished rather than enriched the system. Human expressions, insofar as they are to function as communicative signs, are socially conventionalized signs. This applies to all but a few instinctive expressions, but even these have to be socially censured if they are to acquire a communicative function. The spontaneous expressive signs that Stanislavskij's system of acting reckoned with were therefore not really spontaneous. Instead, they were the unconscious reproduction of communicative behavior of ordinary people in ordinary situations. The actor who was trained to live through the dramatic situation of the character he was going to 'be' on the stage was not to try to control the expressive activity of his face and body, because Stanislavskij wanted to exclude the interference of the consciousness in the process of empathy and expression. The unconscious expressions, however, are not spontaneous, but deep-seated socialized habits whose social origin has been forgotten due to automatization. Thus instead of creating spontaneous signs, the actor would reproduce automatic signs without being aware of this.[12] One might add to Honzl's critique that Stanislavskij's automatic signs lack even the status of artistic signs that the traditional signs of the mimic mask acquired by deliberately selecting, combining and intensifying or diminishing the signs taken from the communicative sign repertoire. By introducing true, real signs in the sense of automatized, everyday communicative signs into the repertoire of theatrical signs, therefore, Stanislavskij ran the risk of destroying the artistic character of the theatrical sign system.

We must now return to our initial question, why Stanislavskij's

[12] *Ibid.*

concept of acting tended to the illusionistic type of theater and to the tragical aspect of Čechov's drama. Now that we have discovered the character of signs underlying Stanislavskij's system of acting, we can formulate the question in the following manner: what has the (pseudo-)spontaneous, true expressive sign of the actor got to do with illusion and tragedy, and to what extent do Čechov's plays need the 'realistic' system of theatrical signs introduced by Stanislavskij? Stanislavskij developed his system of acting under the influence of Čechov's drama. He discovered in Čechov's plays the so called "underwater current" (*podvodnoe tečenie*), which is not identical with the typical ambivalent construction (*podtekst*) of artistic texts, but is rather a consequence of the psychological motivation of the construction of text, proper to the realistic period of writing. The "underwater current" in Čechov's drama means on the one hand a specific attitude of the speakers in dramatic dialogue—the speakers no longer talk about their feelings, intentions, or actions (to others or to themselves), but rather talk n o t about them. Consciously or unconsciously, they avoid communication on the problems they are really concerned about, and try to speak on subjects that do not concern them. Consequently, they avoid dialogical situations in which confrontation with a given partner might force them to make a confession, and seek out conversational situations in which all participants are free to speak about impersonal subjects to disinterested partners. This brings up the above-mentioned phenomenon of the polylogue in Čechov's plays. But the inner situation of the speaker with all its dramatic tension cannot be totally suppressed. Since it is not given room in conscious verbal behavior, it finds expression in unconscious, uncontrolled verbal and non-verbal behaviour. The "underwater current" means on the other hand, therefore, a verbal and non-verbal text structure in drama that is only partly organized by intentional and conscious utterances and behaviour; it is partly organized by non-intentional and unconcious forces which gives the inner emotional life of the speakers away. From the semiotic point of view, the "underwater current" leads to a sign structure according to which the verbal utterances of a dramatic character do not denote his inner life (thoughts and emotions) and actional intentions, but in denoting something else (irrelevant conversational topics), their textual organization provides an insight into what the character is trying not to talk about. This sign structure is therefore linked with the psychological

35

rather than the logical motivation of the text structure; moreover, as the psychological motivation becomes dominant, it favors non-verbal expression before verbal. Thus all in all, in Čechov's dialogues it is less important what the characters talk about than at what moment and how they talk about something or try to avoid talking, and sometimes their interest in apparently insignificant things in a given situation tells more about their life problems than a whole conversation.

Stanislavskij understood well the symptomatic type of signs and the corresponding psychological motivation of the characters' behavior in Čechov's plays. He also understood that the traditional art of acting, which was orientated towards verbally expressed emotions, intentions and actions and left nothing to non-verbal signs but gave everything to rhetorically brilliant monologues and dialogues, was unable to do justice to Čechov's subtle psychological art. Therefore, he taught the actor how to find an inner, emotional relation to the dramatic character and make his body an expressive instrument for his own, personal emotions, which were to correspond to those that the dramatic character felt but did n o t want to express. *Perezivanie* and the psychotechnique of acting were necessary steps in the process of making Čechov's dramas theatrically efficient.

As to Stanislavskij's inclination to illusionistic theatrical art and the genre of tragedy, it is above all his yearning for emotional truth that lies behind it. Illusion, as has already been stated, does not mean that actor and spectator forget the fictive status of the dramatic world represented, but rather that they agree to a convention whereby they accept the represented world as the condition for an emotional process within the actor that is identical with what the actor as a real person would feel if he lived through the dramatic situation in his own life. The actor must therefore bring his whole personality and his life experience into the embodiment of the dramatic character that he is going to 'be' more than represent. From the point of view of the sign-creating activity that the actor performs, the beginning of this activity lies in the acceptance of the psychological and physiological features of the dramatic character and its dramatic situation as conditioning the process of emotional *perezivanie* by the actor. The next phase is then the production of the corresponding symptomatic signs, and the final phase is the reproduction of the inner situation of the dramatic character by the spectator; who, guided by the system of symptomatic signs stemming from the actor, lives through the inner life of the dramatic character as if he were a real, living person. The borderline between the actor as a real person and the dramatic character as an artificial semiotic construction is blurred in this process, not because the spectator forgets the fictive origin of the dramatic charater, but because the actor looses his inner distance to the real *symptomatic* signs that he unconsciously produces through his true emotions. The proximity of this sign process to tragedy may be explained with reference to two points. One of them is the axis of identification between the dramatic character and the spectator which enables the spectator to live through the crisis of that character as if he himself were exposed to it. This axis is formed by the inner, emotional truth behind the outer, symptomatic signs that constitute the scenic image of the dramatic character. The identification in general is necessary to produce the effect of fear and compassion, two of the three elements of the aesthetic experience in tragedy. The same effect is produced by the second point, which lies in the fact that the dramatic characters do not reach their goal of becoming authentic personalities; as in the case of Ivanov, Uncle Vanja, Treplev and even the three sisters, their lifelong endeavor fails to attain any ultimate significance, and they suffer desperately in consequence. The spectator and the actor suffer with them, the first by adopting the inner perspective of the dramatic character on the whole dramatic situation, the second by psychologically becoming the dramatic character himself. In Stanislavskij's system of acting there is even a starting point for the third element of the tragical aesthetic experience which makes up for the catharsis, purification through fear and compassion. It lies in the fact that every actor on the stage has to undergo the process of *preživanie*, regardless of the dramatical importance of the role, of the corresponding character in the action. This creates a multitude of inner situations which the spectator must adopt simultaneously. A polyperspective view on the whole dramatic situation is thereby established which guarantees the spectator a certain distance despite his intense emotional involvement, and distance is one condition for the aesthetic character of the tragical experience. Thus Stanislavskij's system of acting guarantees on the one hand the destruction of the hierarchy among the dramatic characters that is typical of Čechov's plays, and on the other hand it creates a polyperspective viewpoint for the spectator that corresponds on the level of the dialogue.

37

Nevertheless, there is one element vital to aesthetic effect in Čechov's plays which falls outside Stanislavskij's method of acting. This element enhances the spectator's aesthetic distance and reintroduces the element of hierarchy which Čechov himself destroyed on the level of the relationship between the dramatic author and his dramatic characters.[13] The dramatic author is endowed with a monologic voice that enables him to pass final judgement on the characters and disturbs the emotional harmony between the characters and the spectator. It sets the spectator free from compassion and fear and activates his rational activity and his sense of irony and laughter. It is rendered perfectly by Mejerchol'd's system of acting, but never by Stanislavskij's.

Instead of the spontaneous (actually: automatic) symptomatic signs that are totally subordinated to the expression of the inner situation of the dramatic character (and of the actor), Mejerchol'd's system of acting centers on the autonomous sign. It incorporates both the traditional set of signs constituting the mimic mask, and the newly introduced movements of the body taken from circus performing and equilibristics which became important ingredients in the training of the Mejerchol'dian actor. The autonomous sign is always deliberately chosen by the actor and intentionally combined with other such signs by the stage-director. Its relationship to the dramatic character is never stable: it can be symptomatic (with regard to artificially selected aspects of the character to which the sign indirectly points). Instead of the expression of the eyes and the voice, it is now the movement of the body that assumes the position of the dominant in this new system of signs. Each movement that the actor performed involved a double task; one was for the actor himself, who had to find among the repertoire of bodily movements such that were able to attract the attention of the spectator in the surroundings of other movements of himself and other actors, and another one for the spectator, who had to discover the possible meaning of these movements. And since it was the dominant of the sign system, each movement carried not only a meaning of its own, but also attributed possible meanings to all the other sign elements on the stage: things

---

[13] This holds only for the main characters, of course, who are all constructed according to the same principle. The minor characters are psychologically less interesting.

and even elements of the decor signified not only themselves, as did the realistic things and settings in Stanislavskij's theater, but were also given their meaning by the relationship that the body of the actor assumed toward them. Mejerchol'd therefore preferred the constructivist style of the stage in which setting and decoration had no meaning of their own and props were given changing meanings according to the necessities of the play.

The criterion for the autonomous movement was no longer emotional truth but aesthetic attraction (the inner life of the actor lost all importance and his emotional relation to the dramatic character was even considered as an obstacle in Mejerchol'd's art of *predstavlenie*). This included from the very beginning of the act of perception an element of distance which was realized through several factors: 1. There was an inner distance between the actor and his role that enabled him to choose effective movements and that made the spectator aware of the artificiality and arbitrariness of these movements. This inner distance was particularly appropriate when the actor wanted to switch from the set of symptomatic signs to the set of conventional ones, as was necessary to express the relapse of Čechov's heroes into traditional role patterns after their failure to become authentic personalities. 2. In choosing optically attractive movements as communicative signs, the actor also had a certain influence on the meaning of these movements and thereby on the final interpretation of the character and his dramatic role. This created a rational rather than an emotional attitude towards the dramatic character and influenced the attitude of the spectator towards the dramatic hero. The spectator would live and suffer with the hero less than he would criticize him according or in opposition to the critical comments suggested by the actor's interpretation. 3. Accompanying the actor's comment on his character and role was the comment of the stage-director, who finally combined all the individual activities of the actors into one super-sign of the stage. In this final act of the stage-director the formal composition of the whole was much more important than the elements of decor and setting, which were so necessary for Stanislavskij.[14] In this combinatory and composi-

[14] Cf. V. Chalizev, *Drama kak javlenie iskusstva*, Moskva 1978, who makes an interesting comparison between Stanislavskij's and Mejerchol'd's attitudes towards decor, space and composition.

tional activity of the stage-director we recognize the hierarchical author's comment in Čechov's plays. Being given a hidden voice by Čechov especially on the level of the dramatic dialogue (polylogue) and on the level of scenic props, in Mejerchol'd's system of acting and staging it receives a reinforced voice through a multitude of newly invented symbolic things and corresponding movements of the actors, who 'play' in a significant way with these things (*igra vešč'ju*) and through a whole ensemble of compositional devices (for example 'leitmotifs' in music, manipulation in the succession of the scenes, temporal manipulation,[15] changing between dynamic and static scenes, etc.) The strong commentatory intervention of the stage-director into the construction of the theatrical super-sign and its message again activates the perceptive and intellectual capacities of the spectator, but less the emotional ones.

If it is true that the actor in Mejerchol'd's system was given a choice between sets of signs, and that the symptomatic signs were also at his disposal, we must make a reservation, because otherwise one might think that Mejerchol'd had already found the synthesis of his and Stanislavskij's systems of acting. Mejerchol'd favored the arbitrary, conventional symptomatic signs. The muscles of the face and the eyes were often hidden behind an immobile mask, so that a 'natural', 'spontaneous' facial expression was impossible. The mask fixed one dominant feature of the dramatic character, and additional changes were expressed by effects of light and shadow and colors. The 'natural' expressiveness of the voice was also altered through an artificial rhythmical diction and of the accompaniment of instruments. In all these devices the principle of externalization (*vnešnifikacija*), that is, the expression of inner processes by outer means, was evident, and it was combined with the principle of contrast: the dynamics of inner spiritual or emotional changes in the characters was underlined by static poses of the body; by making a rhythmical pause in the stream of movements the actor would become motionless and for a moment offer the spectator the view of a statue.[16]

[15] The tempo of a scene was derived from its emotional weight in the whole structure of the play, so that the feeling for time and rhythm became very subjective.

[16] The technique of changing between movement and immobile poses was used especially effectively in Mejerchol'd's staging of Èrdman's *Mandat*. For the description of this and all the other stagings, see K. L. Rudnickij, *Režisser Mejerchol'd*, Moskva 1978 (English translation: *Meyerhold the Director*, Ann Arbor 1981).

Thus if Stanislavskij's system of acting founded upon the 'natural' symptomatic signs was almost exclusively concentrated on the psychological aspect of Čechov's dramatic characters and made the spectator live with them instead of judging them, Mejerchol'd's system, using openly conventional signs, concentrated likewise exclusively on the non-psychological outer aspect, whereby the spectator was stimulated to laugh at the characters and to judge them along with the actors, the stage-director and finally the dramatic author himself. If we consider the fact that Čechov endows the dramatic author of his plays with a voice superior to the voices of his characters, one might be tempted to say that in stressing the author's voice through his various artistic devices Mejerchol'd is more right than Stanislavskij, who deletes this critical voice totally. On the other hand, however, it cannot be forgotten that the psychological motivation of the characters' verbal and non-verbal behaviour is essential to the textual structure of the plays; in other words, it is only insight into the inner world of the characters that can impart full significance to their utterances and actions. Thus it is the combination of logically exclusive principles such as the inner and the outer view of the dramatic characters, the psychological and artificial motivation of the elements of the dramatic texts, and the anti-hierarchical equality between the speakers of the polylogue and the monological hierarchy of the dramatic author that together contribute to the unique aesthetic value of Čechov's work. This complexity has yet to be reproduced by an adequate theatrical system.

Bochum – Amsterdam

Angela Martini

The Syncretism of Dramatic Structure and the Failure of L. N. Andreev's Dramas

At first glance it may seem that Andreev was not exaggerating when he self-confidently stated that he had made a significant contribution to the regeneration of the Russian drama.[1] His early plays employ the entire gamut of devices that had been discovered and developed since the turn of the century in an effort to free traditional dramatic structures from conventions and patterns which had by then become largely meaningless. Despite the often apparently undramatic nature of these devices, it was felt that they could contribute to the creation of a new dramatic art by transcending the narrow confines of the illusionistic stage and would establish a new relationship to the spectator, who was already now often integrated into the play or at least was provoked by it.

Andreev's works were frequently staged in and outside of Russia, and his plays were discussed by Stanislavskij and Mejerchol'd and by Max Reinhardt in Germany.[2] A closer consideration, however, reveals that Andreev's dramas are short-lived products of the early twentieth century and that his claim was simply unjustified.

Andreev's correspondence with the MChAT producer Nemirovič–Dančenko clearly shows that he was aware of the plurimediality of his plays even as he was writing them. That is, he both conceived of the dramatic text as a text that was to be realized on stage and attempted to duplicate the interaction between author, producer and actor in an interaction between the dramatic play and the audience. Already here, however, we must make a qualitative distinction between the two types of drama that are characteristic of Andreev. On the one hand there is the anti-illusionistic or stylized drama of 1906, 1907 and 1909 (I think that such a designation is more adequate and precise than definitions which seek to label these plays on the basis of

---

[1] "Pis'ma k V.I. Nemirovič-Dančenko", in: *Voprosy teatra*, Moskva 1966, p. 279.
[2] Cf. H.-H. Krause, *Die vorrevolutionären russischen Dramen auf der deutschen Bühne*. Grundzüge ihrer deutschen Bühneninterpretation im Spiegel der Theaterkritik, Emsdetten 1972, p. 167–169.

their content), whose interaction is critical and argumentative and results in a new formulation and use of dramatic devices. On the other, there are the realistic—or, as Andreev preferred to call them, the "panpsychological"—plays.[3] This primarily terminological distinction implies essential shifts on the level of dramatical material, i.e. dramatic composition and *sujet*. The stylized drama is a drama of theses and/or ideas, whereas the "panpsychological" play uses more or less specific, individualized destinies to treat historical and psychological problems and present a critical attitude toward civilization. In the stylized drama of ideas, the dramatic *sujet*, the characters and the action are subordinated to a preconceived idea, and this subordination is intended to stimulate a revalorization of the plane of meaning of the dramatic composition. In the "panpsychological" drama, by contrast, the characters and action lead forward to the statement of an idea, and the composition loses some of its autonomous meaning.

Of Andreev's 21 plays, the stylized ones appear to be isolated experiments whose formal innovations are seldom transferred to his later dramas. His euphoric use of new forms was succeeded by hackneyed devices and mediocrity. The degree of abstraction he had striven toward was too high and all-embracing, and this stylized dramatic form proved to have little immediate impact or fertility. Moreover, as is evident from Andreev's prose, the psychological novel and the new science of psychology increasingly became his literary ideals: the "human soul" and intellect and man's psychological individuality and universality were declared to be the "new hero" of the theater.[4]

In his first stylized drama *The Life of Man* (1906) Andreev—as Mejerchol'd's enthusiasm confirms[5]—seems to have found a way to renovate theatrical form and content. His approach had a practical equivalent in contemporary theories of directing which sought to schematicize the drama and reduce it to its elementary components.[6] Already *The Life of Man* and increasingly the later plays of the same

[3] L. Andreev, *Pis'ma o teatre* (Reprinted from *Literaturno-chudožestvennye al'manachi.* Izd. Šipovnik. Kniga 22. S.-Peterburg 1914) Letchworth 1974, Pis'mo 2.
[4] *Ibid.* Pis'mo 1, p. 8.
[5] Cf. V. E. Mejerchol'd, *Stat'i. Pis'ma. Reči. Besedy*, t. 2, Moskva 1968, p. 232.
[6] Cf. V. Brjusov, "Nenužnaja pravda. Po povodu Moskovskogo Chudožestvennogo teatra", in: *Sobranie sočinenij v semi tomach*, Moskva 1975, t. 6, p. 62–74; also Mejerhol'd, op. cit.

type, however, exhibit conceptual inconsistencies which derive from Andreev's typical lack of balance between intended meaning and dramatic realization. As was soon perceived by Mejerchol'd and Stanislavskij, his syncretistic thinking becomes apparent in the syncretistic form of his plays, and this is probably the main reason why they are no longer staged today.

As is frequently observed, Andreev's stylized drama employs structural elements and means of expression which are reminiscent of antique tragedy, Medieval mystery plays, and the Calderonian Spanish baroque theater. Such devices, however, are merely superficial borrowings and adaptations, and he does not attempt to exploit their semantic implications. Although Andreev strove to break down and overcome the apparently irreconcilable intellectual, political and social dichotomies, what he mainly formulates in his works is the negativity of the status quo rather than the positive possibility of transcending or resolving such conflicts. His undifferentiated Weltanschauung and political point of view prevent him from reasserting the Medieval and baroque concept of "ordo". Unlike the plays of e.g. Paul Claudel and T. S. Eliot, his "mystery play" *The Life of Man* does not represent a "synthesis of Christianity and modernity".[7] Practically the only thing that proved fertile for his stylized drama was the opposition of an epic and a dramatic plane. This created distance and allowed historical yet intentionally transhistorical themes based on individualized examples to be elevated to a generalized, universal level.

The relationship between the stage and the audience gives rise to a fundamental difference between the two types of drama. The stylized drama includes the audience as an active constituent factor, but subsequently the quality of this relationship is exactly reversed. While in his "Letters on the Theater" of 1912 and 1913 Andreev tends to view the relation between stage and audience as being based on naturalistic premises of identification and even refers to Tolstoj's central aesthetic concept of "infectiousness" (*zarazitel'nost'*), in his correspondence with Stanislavskij and Nemirovič−Dančenko around 1906 he emphatically repudiates the infectious drama and the dramatic form of realistic illusion. His main postulate was "to annul

[7] K. Ziegler, "Das deutsche Drama der Neuzeit", in: *Deutsche Philologie im Aufriß* Bd. 2 Berlin 1960 (2. Auflage), p. 2195.

naturalistic representation but retain realistic foundations". And
"... if the stage in Čechov's and even Maeterlinck's case was supposed to represent life, here it should only reflect life. Not for a
moment is the audience allowed to forget that it has a picture before
it, that it is in the theater, and that it is watching actors performing
various roles. Nor must the actors forget during the performance that
they are actors playing to an audience. How can such a relation be
rendered: acting that is at once captivating and artificial; can it be
done at all? I don't know."[8]

Beyond conveying an awareness that the play is a play, Andreev's
attempt to shatter the naturalistic mimetic illusion has a didactic
purpose, in that he tries to communicate new knowledge and provoke
the audience to think. In keeping with this conception—and in contrast to the symbolist drama—realistic, referential connections cannot be abandoned. Although the "real" action is subordinate to the
"action of meaning", fragments of and reference to an identifiable
world of experience must not be eliminated. The interaction that
takes place between a decomposed dramatic form and a narrative
sujet—despite all the alienation strategies implicit in the latter—
corresponds to a dialectic of estrangement and identification on the
part of the audience. This is the consequence of the structure of the
stylized drama, which is defined by the relationship between the
thesis and its illustration, between the proposition and its proof.

The prologues to *The Life of Man*, *King Hunger* and *Anathema*
serve to show that the epic plane, i.e. the plane of ideas, is superior to
the dramatic plane that begins in the first acts. On the one hand, the
linguistic utterances of the prologue characters may belong to the
intermediary communication system only, as in *The Life of Man*. This
is true even though on the dramatic plane the silent presence of
Someone in Gray, who is invisible to the characters, to a certain
extent transcends the communication between the audience and the
action on the stage and thus becomes a symbol of the hopeless
absence of linguistic contact between Man and Fate. The other
alternative is that such utterances may encroach upon the interior
communication system of the dramatic plane. Most consistently in
The Life of Man, these prologue characters function as a commenta-

[8] "Neizdannye pis'ma Leonida Andreeva", in: *Učenye zapiski Tartuskogo univer-
siteta*, vyp. 119, (= Trudy po russkoj i slavjanskoj filologii 5), Tartu 1962, p. 382.

tor and play-leader who links the play to the dramatic plane. The various acts (i.e. pictorial segments) of the dramatic plane, which in *The Life of Man* and *King Hunger* are moreover announced authorially through the use of scene titles, do not develop, but are united and bound into a whole by the prologue characters in accordance with the idea to be illustrated or with a predetermined design in which the individual segments are merely components.

Already in the prologue—and this is most rigorously observed in *The Life of Man*—the allegorized personification of the supernatural forces in control of human destiny foreshadows the course of the drama, naming the stages that will be translated into scenic terms to illustrate their theses. Moreover, the prologue contains the first comments on and interpretations of the subsequent action on the dramatic plane. In *The Life of Man* the "metaphor of life as a play and human existence as a role"[9] is made particularly obvious through the use of a commentator. The fictitiousness of the theater thus becomes a simile of the illusionary quality of everything terrestial, and the stylization and abstraction of the characters into personifications and states of being is consistent with the fact that they are bound to parts that *a priori* preclude human subjectivity and freedom of choice.

King Hunger and *Anathema*, which Andreev explicitly subsumes under the type of drama represented by *The Life of Man*, show that modifications and contradictions have been introduced in this conception of an omniscient play-leader who is ultimately an expression of man's predestination and lack of freedom. The modification is that the prologue has been expanded into an independent scene in which King Hunger and Anathema are provoked by the doubts and opposition of their interlocutors into proving their thesis about man's potential and limitations. Contradictions occur between the semantic and dramatic structures, on the one hand, and their conception, on the other, insofar as the play-leaders no longer serve exclusively as commentators placed on the periphery but are now integrated into the dramatic action. From a semantic point of view this means that conflict situations develop between the prologue characters and the characters of the dramatic plane. Once again the individual scenes show a tendency to develop causally on the basis of a more or less precisely defined conflict situation. Although their sequence is still

[9]W. Hinck, *Das moderne Drama in Deutschland*, Göttingen 1973, p. 117.

47

determined by the play-leader, the introduction and expansion of conflicts also implies a reduction in the stylization of the characters and their actions, and from the viewpoint of reception this in turn diminishes the degree to which the play is unmasked as a play. The shortening of the distance between the play-leader and the play he has set in motion has as its counterpart a reduction in the distance between the action and the audience.

Action as a causally and psychologically motivated sequence of actions and reactions is negated in the stylized drama. Events as a state of being and repetitive uniformity exist outside all personal or interpersonal relationships. This is a consequence of the negation of the individual as a free and autonomous agent. In *The Life of Man* it is expressed by eliminating the dramatic character Man as a dramatic subject, and in *King Hunger* by substituting social groups for the individual, while in *Anathema* it appears in modified form in the relation of dependence between David Lejzer and the prologue character Anathema.

In the realistic, "panpsychological" plays, however, action is defined as the actions and reactions of a character in a particular situation occurring in the context of events comprising the entire text. In most of Andreev's later plays a positive or negative relationship is established between the character who is confessing or speaking and the action. This is true both of socially determined characters whose ability to make an intentional choice is entirely absent or greatly restricted, and of those who intervene in the state of things through some disruptive act.

In the stylized plays, the epic plane of ideas and the schematized stylization of the characters and their context abolish such a relationship between characters and events. Because the plane of ideas is itself already rife with conflicts and contradiction, as soon as its statements become less than absolute and exclusive the principle of stylization is weakened and traditional dramatic devices once again gain the upper hand. This happens, for example, in *King Hunger*, where Time and Death doubt that King Hunger will make good his promise to deliver the starving from their misery, and in *Anathema*, where the allegorical prologue character Anathema questions the absoluteness of God.

Already in *The Life of Man* Andreev proves incapable of maintaining throughout the abstractness of Man, who passes through the stages of life like a marionette or puppet. Both Man's desperate curse (4th picture), which is psychologically motivated by the death of his only son, and the verbal communication of this death serve to breach the distance in the intermediary communication system and destroy the characters' undifferentiated psychological uniformity and total lack of connection within the interior communication system. Andreev was aware of this conceptual inconsistency: "Since all this is merely a reflection, merely a distant and apparent echo, there can be no drama in human life. In the 4th picture, whose prayers and curses make it well suited to purely dramatic phenomena, it was only with difficulty that I managed to refrain from crossing the boundary and depicting in certain places real life instead of a reflection of life. Such an error did creep in, for instance, when Wife enters after the death of their son and asks Man in a single word: 'Dead?'. It is obvious how dramatic and artless (*bezyskusstvenno*) this word can sound. And yet at the same time it destroys the uniformity of the whole. I therefore replaced it with the far more abstract (*otdaljajuščee*) and moderate 'Is our son dead?' "[10]

This is another, increasingly frequent inconsistency which ruptures the form of the stylized drama: the claim to universality is weakened by an individualization and personalization of Fate, which is explained and interpreted through social or psychological motivation. The scenes or individual pictures thus no longer represent ahistorical or all-embracing examples or a reduced and abstracted model of reality, and artificiality as a device of the anti-illusionistic drama is largely eliminated.

Andreev's didactic impulse to provoke reflection on the part of the audience split his anti-illusionistic drama into two planes, thereby giving it a certain resemblance to the dual structure of the parable. But he does not, as is demanded by the parable, develop the thesis and its exemplification and illustration into a synthesis or unambiguously deducible doctrine. The questions which figure in the dramas do not range themselves in any clearly formulizable or formulated *Weltanschauung*. For this reason they "cannot be resolved into any

[10] "Neizdannye pis'ma", p. 383. "To curse, according to Dostoevsky, is the only privilege which differentiates man from other animals and, perhaps, the only means whereby he can 'convince himself that he is a man and not a piano key'." J. B. Woodward, *L. Andreyev. A Study*, Oxford 1969, p. 155.

49

unequivocal, comprehensible meaning: although the relation to reality is still palpable, mediation is no longer guaranteed".[11]

The fluctuating relationship between the thesis and its aesthetic representation, in which references to extra-aesthetic reality are obvious despite stylization, remains fragmentary and unbalanced. Nevertheless, the plays are implicitly didactic. As in Andreev's prose, we are shown man's lack of alternatives in an opaque world whose political and social events cannot be influenced or directed. Unlike Brecht, whose parable plays contain clearly marked attitudes and opinions, Andreev does not show us any change of man and the world by means of or within the play itself. His only aim is to provoke the spectator into a new awareness of reality by presenting it through the use of alienation techniques rather than mimetically. "Trusting in the audience's ability to learn", he demonstrates on the stage "man's inability to learn."[12] As always I ask but do not answer questions, and this must be clearly expressed in the performance."[13]

Thus Andreev aspired to enlighten the audience by asking it to answer questions which he himself was unable to solve. This intention, however, was doomed to founder on the dramatic realization of his abstract subject matter. On the one hand the world is shown to be amenable to criticism, yet on the other it is subject to *a priori* laws. Analogously, man is shown as a puppet in the power of irrationally and empirically incomprehensible forces that preclude him from taking responsibility for and planning his own destiny, yet at the same time he is a victim and a product of himself and society. While the plane of ideas does not admit of any possibility of changing the world by means of social, political or ethical actions, the dramatic plane, without clearly formulating it or allowing it to become a constructive element of the message, hints at such a possibility throughout. In *The Life of Man*, for example, Man's lack of freedom, which is his own fault, emerges increasingly to the fore and replaces the theme of fatalistic predestination. The loss of identity and subjectivity which he inflicts upon himself in his quest for power and riches comes to a climax in the ball scene: "In general, this ball is meant to demonstrate

---

[11] K.-D. Müller, "Das Ei des Kolumbus? Parabel und Modell als Dramenformen bei Brecht-Dürrenmatt-Frisch-Walser (Originalbeitrag)", in: W. Keller (ed.), *Beiträge zur Poetik des Dramas*, Darmstadt 1976, p. 443 f.

[12] Hinck, *op. cit.*, p. 176.

[13] "Neizdannye pis'ma", p. 385.

the vanity of glory, wealth and so called happiness ... It is not a satire. It is an illustration of how sated people, whose souls are dead, amuse themselves."[14] Here, to emphasize his intent, Andreev introduces the grotesque and reifies his characters. Such devices, however, are mainly used to characterize the musicians and ball guests, while Man himself is present at first only in the remarks of the latter and then appears as a silent figure on the stage.[15] The fact that Man is excepted from reification and the grotesque may be one reason why he is less stylized in the 4th picture.

The discrepancy in content, style and form between the two planes becomes even greater in *King Hunger* and *Anathema*. The extensively stylized plane of ideas, which by means of reduction and abstraction only brings out the basic structure of the idea on stage, stands in opposition to the dramatic plane, which is by now particularized and detailed. Andreev deviates more and more from the postulate which he considered indispensible to the staging of these plays, namely that "characters, situations and scenery should lead up to the fundamental ideas, simplified and at the same time be made more profound by the absence of details and secondary phenomena".[16]

The plane of ideas and the stylization based upon it are no longer superimposed on the dramatic plane so as to give direction to the whole, and the dramatic plane increasingly acquires its own dynamics. Although the prologue still serves as the starting point for the pictures which follow, their sequence and semantic content are comprehensible enough without any prologue at all. The prologue and the deliberate separation of a plane of ideas, therefore, become mere formal devices.

In the first picture of *King Hunger*, the gestures and language of the workers are still a stylized expression and illustration of the opposition between violence and non-violence and of the reduction and deformation of man by the machine. In the subsequent pictures, however, the opposition between master and slave is resolved in such a way that it is no longer the *state* of things as such that is primarily

---

[14] *Ibid.*, p. 383.
[15] H.−B. Harder, "Die tragische Farce − Zum Grotesken im Drama Bloks und Andreevs", in: *Sinn oder Unsinn? Das Groteske im modernen Drama*, Basel-Stuttgart 1965, p. 147−170.
[16] "Neizdannye pis'ma", p. 389.

demonstrated; instead, it is the effects of this sort of social tension that are shown, often parodically. King Hunger's declaration that this time he intends to allow the rebellion of the poor to triumph is no longer necessary to an understanding of the dramatic plane.

Besides being conceived as stylized personifications of states of beings and functions, we find now that dramatic characters are increasingly portrayed as types related to a particular social context. If the relatives and neighbors in *The Life of Man* are still a stylized expression of general moral attitudes and emotions such as hate, envy, jealousy, etc., the poor in *King Hunger* are differentiated as the types of the alcoholic, the criminal driven by hunger, and the innocent whore. A historically indeterminate collective totality that absolutizes the human condition is superseded by differentiation and specifications. The grotesque and its alienating effects are largely replaced by satire and parody.

In *Anathema* the plane of ideas is integrated into the dramatic plane through the not entirely harmonious relationship between the prologue character Anathema and the already individualized dramatic subject Lejzer; it loses some of its function as an intermediary between the play and the audience, as the play-leader Anathema is by no means only an autonomous and subordinate character. The stylization of the characters and situations on the dramatic plane is reduced; figurative and linguistic portrayal is now determined by Lejzer's uncertainties and inconsistencies. Although the prologue still functions as a plane that creates distance, on the dramatic plane the play is enriched by conflicts and events which once again restore illusion and suspense as dramatic elements.

The existence of the two planes in these plays is underlined, albeit inconsistently, by the use of language. There is a striking stylistic difference between the prologue and the dramatic plane. The acting and language of the allegorical prologue characters are the *Gestus* and reference point of the idea. Their language is rhetorical, its function is appellative, and it is permeated by an elevated stylistic pathos, all of which is quite in keeping with the abstract themes of their utterances. Thus the "poetic" stylization in *King Hunger*, consisting of rhetorical questions, parallel syntactic constructions, identical and anaphoric repetitions, and rhytmicized lines and songs, serves to stress both the artificiality and the meaning of these passages. The contrived nature of the characters and their statements manifests itself not only in the "what" but also in the "how" of their speech. This principle, however, is restricted already in *King Hunger*, and becomes even more so in *Anathema*.

Here, because the characters are assailed by doubts and attempt to vindicate themselves, we are given the "why" as well as the "what". Unlike Someone in Gray (*The Life of Man*) King Hunger and Anathema no longer represent absolute ideas, but rather stand for points of view whose veracity is confirmed or denied on the dramatic plane. This results in a curve of suspense that rises toward the end, and once again the anti-illusionistic principle is reduced.

The rhetorical language of the stylized drama, however, is not only characteristic of the plane of ideas, but also asserts itself on the dramatic plane whenever a character rebels against Fate or tries to come to terms with a challenging situation. At times the language used is determined by the pathos of the situation, while at others the characters speak their mind in an attempt to convince someone or to avoid ambiguity. An intimation of altercations, which at times mark an overlapping of the plane of ideas and the dramatic plane (*Anathema*), alters not only the characters but also their speech and the dialogue, taking the form of an unconnected series of lines. To a certain extent the dialogue in such places acquires intentional and actional elements, and no longer serves primarily as a means for generalizing and objectivizing characters and situations.

How often such proclamations and statements are in danger of becoming mechanical catchwords is even more obvious in Andreev's non-stylized plays, in which the artificiality of the exaggerated rhetoric and pathos violates what was intended to be the naturalistic logic of the dialogue.

The linguistic structure of the stylized drama is expanded by means of choric groups whose language accords with their conception as representatives of situations and states of being. They are rarely given any function beyond that, and although Andreev regarded his choric ensembles as following the tradition of the antique chorus,[17] they seldom fulfill its role of interpreting and intermediating between the dramatic plane and the audience. His choruses do not leave "the narrow sphere of action in order to expatiate upon things past and

[17] A. N. Andreev, "Iz vospominanij o L. Andreeve", in: *Krasnaja Nov'*, 1926:9, p.214 f.

things to come, upon distant times and people, on humanity at large in order to draw the great conclusions of life and voice the lessons of wisdom".[18] It is their referential and informational linguistic attitude that is paramount; only occasionally are they given the function of a commentator (the Old Woman and Old Women in *The Life of Man*). One of the reasons why Andreev misinterpreted and refashioned his choruses seems once again to derive from his inability or refusal to provide clear answers or at least an intimation of his opinions and attitudes. Another may be seen in the fact that his choric groups rarely refer back to the plane of ideas, nor do they stand in a relation of epic superiority to the characters or the situations of the dramatic plane. The function of his choruses, therefore, is fundamentally different from those of Brecht. In Brecht's plays the chorus can demonstrate the "correct attitude"; it can invite the spectator "to form opinions, to summon his own experiences to help him, to exercise control. Such choruses appeal to the practical man in the spectator and call upon him to emanicipate himself *vis à vis* both the represented world and the representation itself."[19]

The dialogic structure of the Andreev chorus is characterized by stasis, a stereotyped repetition of phrases, and a synonymous expansion and arbitrary and associative ordering of lines. These features are semantic and formal expressions of the absolute lack of personal relations within the group and among the individual characters and represent an amplification of the phenomenon of "talking at cross purposes".

Both the characters and their spoken lines lack distinctive individual features. One immediate expression of this is the way in which a single sentence or thought is often distributed among several speakers. At such times language becomes autonomous, as it is not bound to any particular point on the dramatic plane: "It is no longer the expression of an individual expecting an answer, but renders the mood common to all".[20]

One cannot avoid the conclusion that Andreev could not really cope with the form of the stylized drama, although his works antici-

[18] F. Schiller, "Über den Gebrauch des Chors in der Tragödie", in: *Goethe, Schiller über das Theater*, Berlin 1949, p. 372.

[19] A. Wirth, "Über die stereometrische Struktur der Brechtschen Stücke", in: R. Grimm (ed.), *Episches Theater*, Köln-Berlin 1966, p. 198.

[20] P. Szondi, *Theorie des modernen Dramas*, Frankfurt 1956, p. 50.

pate individual elements in the theater of Majakovskij, Brecht, and the Expressionists. The main reason for this is that Andreev was an intuitive rather than intellectual writer. Well versed in the works of modern dramatists such as Ibsen, Čechov and Maeterlinck, he sensed that the new devices employed by them could prove effective for a semantic extension of the theater, but he was himself unable to maintain the proper intellectual and aesthetic balance. He had attempted a formal experiment in which the thematic matter was to become form, but he was forced to fall back upon traditional form in order to return autonomy to his thematic matter. Even plays like *Black Masks, The Ocean,* etc., which use numerous alienation effects, represent merely a transitional stage between the stylized dramas and the "panpsychological" plays. In his last one-act play *Requiem* (1916), however, Andreev once again departs from the realistic mode to stage the breakdown of the theater: the stage is empty, no play is performed, and the spectators are wooden puppets. Could this perhaps be a requiem for his own plays?

Cologne

Lars Kleberg

Vjačeslav Ivanov and the Idea of Theater

At first glance it might seem puzzling to talk about the Russian symbolist theoretician Vjačeslav Ivanov's "idea of theater" and even to make him represent a certain "concept of theater" comparable with others, like naturalism or "conventionalism".[1] After all, Ivanov's writings related to theater consist of two scholary works on the Dionysian Mysteries, two plays that have never been performed, and a couple of articles about theater or drama where not one single company, director or actor is ever mentioned. With these sources at hand, can one really talk about Ivanov's concept of theater? In this paper I will argue that one can do so on a certain level of abstraction. A closer look at the poet and critic's involvement in the theatrical movements before and after the revolution, however, convinces one that using the formula "Ivanov's idea of theater" one should stress the word *idea* rather than the word *theater*. But in this sense, Ivanov's importance for early 20th century Russian theater aesthetics seems unquestionable.

Vjačeslav Ivanovič Ivanov (1866–1949) was the foremost theoretician of the Russian symbolists. He belonged to the so-called younger generation of symbolists, together with Andrej Belyj and Aleksandr Blok. If the "older" symbolists had been concentrating on a purely aesthetical reaction against naturalism in art and positivism in world-view, the younger symbolists would agree that art was not only concerned with the Beautiful, but with the Good and the True as well. This triad—the True, the Good and the Beautiful—evidently refers to Platonism. Neo-platonism in the interpretation of the German romantics and the philosophy of Vladimir Solov'ev were, in fact, the main ideological sources of the younger symbolists.

The impact of the German tradition on Ivanov was very strong. As Sergej Averincev says, Ivanov was as far away from the "aestheticism and dandyism of London as from the Parisian decadence of the *fin de*

---

[1] Cf. the typology of stage-audience relations in Russian theater in Lars Kleberg, *Teatern som handling. Sovjetisk avantgardeestetik 1917–1927*, Stockholm 1977, pp. 66–74, and Olle Hildebrand's analysis in *Harlekin Frälsaren. Teater och verklighet i Nikolaj Evreinovs dramatik*, Uppsala 1978, pp. 24–33.

siècle".[2] Through the German romantics' philosophy of the national spirit, encoded in the cultural texts and primarily in the national language itself, Ivanov also came close to the Neoslavophile movement, firmly believing, through all the crises of the 20th century, in the mission of Russia interpreted in religious-mystical terms.

It is in this general context Ivanov's aesthetics and his idea of theater should be seen. The most important intellectual influence on Ivanov was no doubt Friedrich Nietzsche and his re-interpretation of the Greek tragedy. Vjačeslav Ivanov was himself a scholar with an extremely wide horizon, having studied with the famous professor Th. Mommsen in Berlin in the 1890's. In a way, one can say that he pursued the same career as Nietzsche—from academic classical philology to the philosophy of culture on the border between science and poetry. Nietzsche's concept of the Greek tragedy and its sources in the Dionysian element of the chorus became decisive for Ivanov's development. The echo of Nietzsche can be heard in almost all Ivanov's writings, from his scholarly works to his poetry. This does not mean, however, that Ivanov was echoing Nietzsche. In fact, he was rather concerned with the problem of *overcoming Nietzsche,* his anti-religious concept and his individualism, by reformulating his very questions and by answering them in a religious and collectivist spirit.[3]

In Ivanov, as in Nietzsche, the student of the past and the prophet co-exist. Ivanov pointed out the crisis of contemporary art: but the crisis was also a promise of a new synthetic epoch, when "intimate" art, refined but isolated, would be replaced by grand collective creation, already prepared by the "monastic" symbolists who were "apparently isolated but basically united with the world, people not with a personal but a universal will".[4] Aestheticism had offered no solution to the crisis. The solution, Ivanov meant, was in "the synthetic art of the pandemic happening (*vsenarodnoe dejstvo*) and the choral drama",[5] where every man would become an active participant.

[2] V. Ivanov, *Stichotvorenija i poèmy*, L. 1976, p. 11.

[3] As V. M. Papernyj points out in his article "Blok i Nicše", it was only the concept of Dionysos that interested Ivanov in Nietzsche, *Trudy po russkoj i slavjanskoj filologii*. XXXI (= *Tartu riikliku ülikooli toimetised*, 491), Tartu 1979, p. 90.

[4] "Predčuvstvija i predvestija", in V. Ivanov, *Po zvezdam, Stat'i i aforizmy*, SPB 1909, p. 197.

[5] *ibid.*

The writings of Vjačeslav Ivanov are highly consistent, in fact being variations on different levels and different tonalities of the same basic theme: the coming of Synthesis. If one makes a periodization of Ivanov's work, it would be based on the context which emphasizes one aspect or the other of the same totality of ideas rather than on some intrinsic turning points in his evolution (in this, Ivanov differs from his colleagues like Belyj or Blok).[6] Having this in mind, one can still tentatively point out five periods in Ivanov's work:

1890's—1904: Academic studies and travels in Europe.

1904—1907: Debute as a poet and critic, return to Russia. The period of "mystical anarchism" and expectation of imminent spiritual revolution or "synthesis".

1907—1910's: Further reinterpretation of Russian culture as a whole in regligious-mystical terms but without immediate escatological perspectives.

1917—1919: In the years of revolution, Ivanov sees an age of Synthesis coming closer again. He becomes involved in the theatrical policies of the new state for a short while.

1920's: As a professor in Baku, Ivanov returns to the studies of antiquity and the origins of Dionysian religion. After the emigration to Rome in 1924, he publishes very little.

Ivanov presented his interpretation of the Dionysian myths for the first time in a series of public lectures for Russians in Paris in 1903 and in print as *The Hellenic Religion of the Suffering God* in 1904.[7] As the title suggests, Ivanov's first work on the Dionysian theme was basically devoted to the religious sources of the Greek tragedy. In fact, Ivanov's main objection to Nietzsche's reconstruction was "its exposition of Dionysian phenomena in purely aesthetic terms".[8] Ivanov's purpose was exactly the opposite: to point out the collective religious essence of tragedy and the necessity for a revival of religious mystical feeling in order for contemporary art to break the "intimate"

---

[6] Çf. Averincev, op. cit., pp. 38—39.
[7] *Ellinskaja religija stradajuščego boga* was published in *Novyj put'* in 1904 and in two issues of *Voprosy žizni* in 1905. The study never appeared as a book, although it was announced several times, e.g. on the back cover of *Po zvezdam* in 1909. Fausto Malcovati pointed out the importance of *Ellinskaja religija . . .* in a paper delivered at the Ivanov symposium at Yale University in 1981 (in print).
[8] "Ellinskaja religija . . .", *Novyj put'* 1904:2, quoted from James West, *Russian Symbolism. A study of Vyacheslav Ivanov and the Russian symbolist aesthetic*, London 1970, p. 100.

or "monastic" limitations and become truly "synthetic". This programme was developed further in a series of important essays published in 1904 in the symbolist organ *Vesy* (*Libra*). In one of these, "New Masks", the focus was especially on the aesthetics of contemporary theater and drama.

In the opening paragraph of "New Masks" Ivanov says that there is one realm of the arts where the need for a revival is felt by almost everyone—that of the stage. "As a matter of fact, the old stage almost does not 'infect' any more—and, most important, it does not *transform* the spectator / . . . /".[9] At the same time the theater has a special potential force to reunite the Poet and the Crowd, the artist and the collective, because of its sources in the cult. For centuries, however, the connection with these collective sources has been suppressed: "the mask has become more and more clearly separated and dense"[10] and the split between protagonist and collective—symbolized by the flood-lights—has grown deeper. But the new drama, Ivanov says, hints at the the possibility of a new dithyrambic unity, which can be a shift to "the opposite pole", that of dithyrambic ecstacy, attained in the collective "choral body".[11] Evidently, the two poles correspond to the Apollo-Dionysos opposition.

What was the essence of this utopian concept of cultic theater, compared with existing forms of performance? In the terms of semiotics, theater can be distinguished from other types of collective performances by two features: the sign function of the performance and the interrelation between stage and audience. On the one hand, theater is distinguished from performances like sport, circus etc. by the reduction or elimination of the sign function in those activities, whereas the difference between actors and spectators is preserved. On the other hand, theater is also distinguished from another related but different activity, the cultic ritual, by the reduction or elimination of the difference between those acting and those watching, while the symbolic (sign) function of the activity is predominant.[12] Ivanov's program propagated the restoration of the cultic principles, which theater—as is usually agreed—has abandoned, thus becoming a secularized art form. The fact that the elimination of the border

[9] *Po zvezdam*, p. 54.
[10] *ibid.*, p. 56.
[11] *ibid.*, p. 57.
[12] Cf. Hildebrand, *op. cit.*, p. 14.

between stage and audience, in principle, implied the elimination of theater as such did not occupy Ivanov. In theater as an art form he was interested in a *shift of emphasis* from the "spectacle" towards the cult. Ivanov developed his concept of the reborn "Dionysian" theater, which he called "collective happening" (*sobornoe dejstvo*) in other essays the following years. In the years of revolutionary emotion and "mystical anarchism", Ivanov's plea for a revival of the collective, cultic element in theater had not only religious but also strong political implications, coming close to the young Wagner's utopia of the all uniting *Volkstheater*.[13] The abolishing of the dualism between actors and audience became a metaphor for the synthetic elimination of a series of other contradictions like Poet vs. Crowd, individualism vs. collectivism, etc. In "Premonitions and Forebodings" (1906), Ivanov declared:

> The theater should once and for all reveal its dynamic essence; thus it should stop being "theater" in the sense of "spectacle" only. No more spectacles, we need no *circenses*. We want to gather in order to create—"act"—collectively, not only watch: "*zu schaffen, nicht zu schauen*". No more play-acting, we want action. The spectator should become an agent, a participant in the action. The crowd of spectators should unite in the body of the chorus, like the mystical community of ancient "orgies" and "mysteries".[14]

Thus the reconstruction of the Dionysian religion as the base for the Greek tragedy of a few years earlier reveals itself as a program for the revival of contemporary theater, and through theater of society. The future of the theater and the future of society were in fact, according to Ivanov's vision, interdependent, the collective cultic theater becoming "the authentic expression of the will of the people".[15]

For Ivanov, this reborn Dionysian theater was a metaphor for the general cultural revival he was prophesizing. In fact, everything he wrote—also his essays—was basically symbolical or metaphorical,

---

[13] Cf. Bernice Glatzer Rosenthal, "Theater as Church: The Vision of the Mystical Anarchists", *Russian History/Histoire Russe* 1977: 2, pp. 122–141; Lars Kleberg, " 'People's Theater' and the Revolution", in N. Å. Nilsson (ed.), *Art, Society, Revolution: Russia 1917–1921*, Stockholm 1979, pp. 179–197.

[14] *Po zvezdam*, p. 206–206.

[15] *ibid.*, p. 219.

always corresponding to his general mythic understanding of existence. Aleksandr Blok at one moment, in 1907, said that he saw Ivanov's *Weltanschauung* as pure poetry.[16] But considering the reciprocity of the relation symbol—reality in Russian symbolism one has to add that, on the other hand, the poetry of Ivanov could be said to be pure *Weltanschauung*. In the case of Ivanov and the idea of theater, one could probably say that if cultic theater was a metaphor for existence, existence was equally a metaphor for the cultic theater of total synthesis. Thus the chorus in the last movement of Beethoven's *Ninth Symphony*, Wagner's *Tristan and Isolde* and Skrjabin's *Poem of Ecstacy* were not only metaphors illustrating the general idea of the synthesis for Vjačeslav Ivanov—they were actual realization of utopia, elements of the future in the present.[17]

Ivanov's equally abstract and suggestive program for the revival of the theater was widely discussed. The notion that the uniting of stage and audience was the solution to the crisis of contemporary theater almost became a cliché. In the important collection of essays *Theater. A Book on the New Theater* (1908)—that the conservative critic N. I. Nikolaev characterized as "a manifesto of theatrical revolution"[18]— several contributions referred to the Wagnerian-Nietzschean concept of tragedy in general and to Ivanov specifically. Although the symbolist himself did not participate in the volume, it was edited by his "mystical anarchist" ally, Georgij Čulkov, who also contributed a paraphrase of the more ethical-political aspect of Ivanov's concept. Only one contributor to the miscellany, Andrej Belyj, was openly negative to the idea of "cultic" theater (as he was, in general, to the "mystical anarchism"), stating that as long as there was no common

---

[16] In a letter to Andrej Belyj dated August 6, 1907: "Vjač. Ivanova cenju, kak pisatelja obrazovannogo i glubokogo i kak prekrasnogo poěta, mirovozzrenie že ego ('mifotvorčestvo') vosprinimaju kak liriku", A. Blok, *Sobranie sočinenij*, t. 8, M.–L. 1963, p. 190.

[17] Here lies the main difference between romantic dualism—based on a static division between the trivial reality and the unattainable ideal—and symbolist dualism, where the symbolical is real and reality symbolical, i.e., where the plane of content suddenly can function as the plane of expression and vice versa. Cf. Z. G. Minc, "Ponjatie teksta i simvolistskaja ěstetika", *Materialy vsesojuznogo simpoziuma po vtoričnym modelirujuščim sistemam*, 1 (5), Tartu 1974, p. 135.

[18] *Teatr. Kniga o novom teatre*, SPB 1908. Nikolaev's criticism is found in his book *Efemeridy*, Kiev 1912, pp. 275–294.

faith uniting society, all discussions about cultic theater was nothing but rhetoric.[19] The reactions to Ivanov's theories from the practical theater workers, even from those belonging to the modernist camp, was ambiguous. The poet's criticism of the existing theater was very general, and when he pointed out elements of the theater of the future already traceable in the present, the examples were taken from music (Beethoven) or drama (Ibsen) or from the synthesis of both (Wagner) but not from the contemporary stage. Directors critical to established theatrical practice (traditional conventionalism as well as the naturalism of Moscow Art Theater) could therefore hardly get any practical impulses from Ivanov's utopian program, which ultimately implied the the dissolution of theater as know till then.

Vsevolod Mejerchol'd was no doubt the the Russian director at the time who had the closest contacts with Ivanov. Having left the Moscow Art Theater in autumn 1905 after the interrupted experiments with symbolist productions at the Theater Studio, Mejerchol'd had moved to Petersburg and soon come in contact with Ivanov and Čulkov. In the beginning of 1906, plans were disussed by the three to start a new theater, called "Torches", like the "mystical anarchists" calender, but the project never progressed further.[20] Mejerchol'd no doubt was attracted by certain aspects of Ivanov's theories, but his famous productions at Vera Komissarževskaja's theater the following season were, although mystical in tone, contemplative rather than "dithyrambic", and the division between stage and audience strongly underlined by the flat stage designs and the stylized speech and movements of the actors.

---

[19] Čulkov's contribution was entitled "Principy teatra buduščego", that of Belyj's "Teatr i sovremennaja drama".

[20] On January 3, 1906, the project of organizing the "Torches" theater was discussed at a meeting in Ivanov's home, where Ivanov talked on the theater of Dionysos, Čulkov on mystical anarchism in the theater, and Mejerchol'd on the technique of the new theater, cf. Blok, op. cit., p. 576. The project never progressed any further. In the autumn of 1906, however, Mejerchol'd became director at Vera Komissarževskaja's theater in the new premises on Oficerskaja street. Before the opening of the season, Komissarževskaja and Mejerchol'd arranged three literary evenings for specially invited guests, poets and artists, where something of the spirit of the earlier theater project may have been preserved. Thus, on October 21, young actors and actesses read Ivanov's *Dithyramb* in the light of torches. Cf. K. Rudnickij, "V teatre na Oficerskoj", *Tvorčeskoe nasledie V. E. Mejerchol'da*, M. 1978, p. 143.

Mejerchol'd's contribution to the 1908 miscellany, "On the History and Technique of Theater", was mainly a defense of the director's "static" symbolist productions, although references were made to Ivanov's appeal for a return to the ancient sources of theater (here understood mainly as an aesthetical and technical problem). In practice, Mejerchol'd at the time of the publication of the collective "manifesto of a theatrical revolution" had clearly pointed out his own principles for the future: a reborn theater of the grotesque, drawing on different theatricalist traditions (especially *commedia dell'arte*), the first example of which had been the production of Blok's *The Fairground Booth* (*Balagančik*) presented already in december 1906. Thus, verbally paying all due respect to the authority of Ivanov, Mejerchol'd in practice wanted to revive theater through the confrontation of the *cabotin* and the audience of the marketplace rather than through reviving the solemn unity of actors and audience.[21] But for the continuous discussion of the conditions of contemporary theater, Vjačeslav Ivanov nevertheless remained an important point of reference for the director in the years to come.

This takes us to another aspect of Ivanov's influential rôle in the life of Russian modernism: the literary symposia of the salon associated with his name. Soon after returning from Europe, in autumn 1905, Ivanov and his wife Lidija Zinov'eva-Annibal had organized a literary salon in their flat facing the Taurida Garden—the so-called "tower". The "Ivanov Wednesdays" quickly became an important forum where members of the Petersburg artistic intelligentsia met for discussions, readings, etc. In the free atmosphere of the "tower", all topics and points of view were equal and in a sense interchangeable without the form of the symposium being disturbed. The "Wednesdays", in the eyes of the participants, were a kind of "spiritual laboratory" for new ideas but even more, perhaps, for a new and universal man, liberated from the the dualism of the world and, of course, from the limitations of everyday life. In this sense, the style of behaviour of the "Tower" in itself had a utopian aspect: it was the realization of "tomorrow" under the conditions of an exclusive,

---

[21] On the striking difference between theory and practice in Mejerchol'd, cf. K. Rudnickij, *Režisser Mejerchol'd*, M. 1969, pp. 76–78, and T. Rodina, *A. Blok i russkij teatr načala XX veka*, M. 1972, p. 78.

"laboratory-like" milieu.[22]
Theater was, naturally, a frequent topic and point of departure for the meetings in the "Tower". Vsevolod Mejerchol'd was one of the frequent participants in the discussions, and it was he who, in 1910, organized a little theatrical performance in the flat of the Ivanovs which has become legendary both in the director's own biography and in the history of the "Tower" and therefore deserves a somewhat closer look.

On April 19, 1910, in the evening, invited guests—friends of the family and close supporters of the "Tower"—gathered at Ivanov's home to witness the first and only performance of the "Tower Theater". The initiative came from Ivanov's step-daughter and some of her teen-age friends. So far the enterprise would seem to be an ordinary family divertissement. In the intimate form, however, something more ambitious was embedded.

The play chosen was nothing less than Calderón's *La devoción de la cruz*, a religious baroque drama, translated by Bal'mont as *Poklonenie krestu*. Although the actors were the young Ivanovs and friends of the "Tower", including the poets Michail Kuzmin and Vladimir Pjast, the director and the stage artist were two of the most famous names in the Russian symbolist theater, Mejerchol'd and Sergej Sudejkin. The play was put on in Ivanovs' dining room with no stage and the simplest possible technical solutions. Instead of making a traditional decor, Sudejkin arranged large pieces of cloth in different deep colors; the lighting consisted of candels in big candelabras. The curtain was replaced by draperies, pulled aside by two young "Moors" and the actors could enter the "stage" from another room through the auditorium.

Afterwards, the critic Znosko-Borovskij published a detailed description of the performance in the modernist journal *Apollon*, a fact which of course once more stressed the importance ascribed to the event by those present.[23] The critic explained that the performance of the "Tower Theater" was an experiment in reviving the form of the

[22] On the style of the "Tower" symposia cf. N. Berdjaev, "Ivanovskie sredy", in S. A. Vengerov (ed.), *Russkaja literatura XX veka. 1890–1910*, t. 3, vyp. 8, M. 1916, p. 97–100; idem, *Dream and Reality. An Essay in Autobiography*, London 1950, pp. 155–162; F. Stepun, *Vstreči*, Mjunchen 1962, pp. 141–144; Carin Tschöpl, *Vjačeslav Ivanov. Dichtung und Dichtungstheorie*, München 1968, pp. 25–48.

[23] E. Znosko-Borovskij, "Bašennyj teatr", *Apollon* 1910:8, pp. 31–36; cf. also the memoirs of one of the participants, V. Pjast, *Vstreči*, L. 1924.

religious Spanish theater. The goal was not, however, a historically true "outward" reconstruction but a reestablishing of the close relation between stage and audience that had existed in Spain more than two hundred years ago. This relation was understood as a spontaneous perception of the spiritual content of the play across the deliberatly conventional language of the stage. The expression on the stage, i.e. the stylized historical reconstruction, was thus only a means to reach the content level where the minds of both spectators and actors should unite. The intentions corresponded to the ideas for the revival of the theater that Ivanov had been advocating.[24]

Although the performance of *La devoción de la cruz* thus was based on certain principles of the cultic theater, especially that of the solemn unity of actors and audience, it had, at the same time, a play-like character. The attempt to put the ideas of cultic theater into practice in the dining room of the "Tower", was no doubt, half joke half serious. The ambiguity of the enterprise was stressed by Vjačeslav Ivanov in a poem where he addressed all the participants in turn in the style of a graceful occasional verse. On the other hand, the poem was entitled "Choromnoe dejstvo" ('Temple Act'), and in the final lines the participants of the "Tower Theater" performance—actors, stage managers and audience together—were called a "Bacchian congregation", i.e. participants in a Dionysian mystery. If Ivanov in the poem referred to his own high-strung concepts with a smile, the divertissement in its turn was elevated to a new level of significance.[25]

In fact, the atmosphere of the "Tower" in 1910 was already different from that of the revolutionary years 1905—1907. That last year, Ivanov's wife Zinov'eva-Annibal had died and the "Wednesdays" had been discontinued to be revived only on a smaller scale in 1910—1911. The time of "mystical anarchism" was past, and in the theater of Mejerchol'd, static symbolism, as mentioned, had been replaced by strong theatricalism (viz. the "Moor" stage hands) which

---

[24] Calderón's play had been pointed out by the critic Merežkovskij already in 1891 as an exemplary drama from the time when theater was still in contact with religious cult; cf. Merežkovskij, *Polnoe sobranie sočinenij*, t. XVII, M. 1914, p. 85.—Ivanov makes a similar reference to Calderón as the last representative, in the past, of cultic drama in *Borozdy i meži*, M. 1916, p. 273.

[25] "Choromnoe dejstvo", *Stichotvorenija i poèmy*, p. 243—244.

was to become the trade-mark of "Doctor Dapertutto".[26]

When returning to theme of the crisis of theater in the following years, Vjačeslav Ivanov never changed his views on the revival of the cultic element in the theater as the solution. Naturally, the political, "anarchist" ring of the declarations of 1905 disappeared, but the basic point was the same. The renaissance of theater as an art form uniting artists and people was for Ivanov not a matter of aesthetic reforms but of re-establishing the bounds with the religious sources of the art. This view was of course quite out of tune with the excessive experiments in theatricalism carried out by people like Mejerchol'd, Tairov and Evreinov and with the development of the so-called little forms, both tendencies characteristic of the pre-war years. In a public lecture in 1914, Ivanov summed up his feeling of alienation. We have the theater we deserve, he said, and cannot have anything else because of the extreme individualism in the surrounding Russian society. Maybe a change will come soon, Ivanov continued:

> But to guess about the future is not worth while. One should not guess about the future, but create for the the future, even if the creation has to be kept for better times, for times when the theater will reveal the the power it has stored through the ages and realize its religious idea.[27]

Not surprisingly, Ivanov belonged to those in Russia who saw the First World War as a trial or a fire, from which Russia would resurrect to a new existence. In this context, tragedy and the idea of the all-unifying cultic theater once again became topical. During the war, Ivanov frequently lectures and writes on the rise of a new "synthetic" culture, clearly locating it in the Slavic world as opposed to Germany as well as France and Britain. Collectivism, according to Ivanov, is something essentially Slavic; the word *sobornost'* could not even be translated adequately into any Western language.[28] As a matter of fact, in a speech given in Moscow in October 1917, Ivanov stated not only that Slavs were "Dionysian" in a metaphorical sense as opposed

---

[26] Serving at the same time as a director at the Imperial theaters in Petersburg, Mejerchol'd in August 1910, under the pseudonym of Doctor Dapertutto, opened his studio "The House of Intermedies" for the public with a pantomime in " Italian" style, *The Scarf of Colombine,* cf. Rudnickij, *Režisser Mejerchol'd,* p. 129–130.

[27] *Borozdy i meži,* p. 278.

[28] *Rodnoe i vselenskoe,* M. 1917, p. 45.

to the "Apollonian" Western Europeans, but that the religion of Dionysos had its origins among the Balkan Slavs, and that Nietzsche's Slavic blood had been far from coincidental for his interest in the Dionysian cult.[29]

Vjačeslav Ivanov was of course negative to the Bolshevik takeover. On the other hand, he was also critical towards the rôle of the Russian intelligentsia before the revolution and strongly on the side of the spontaneous popular movements whenever he could see them as steps towards the realization of the ideal of *sobornost'*. In the autumn of 1918, the poet started working with the new revolutionary government, becoming head of the "historical-theoretical section" of the Moscow Theater Department (TEO) of the Commissariat of Enlightenment. During 1919 Ivanov read a series of important lectures, wrote articles and played an active role in the work of the People's Commissariat.[30]

Already in the first issue of *Vestnik Teatra* (*Theater Herald*), the journal of TEO, one could find a detailed report on the first of a series of lectures that Ivanov had initiated at the artists' club "The Red Cock". The lectures on the origins of Greek tragedy and the development of tragedy in European literature were followed by several others where he once again pointed out the two composers who had laid the foundations for the revival of the synthetic "people's theater" to come: Wagner and Skrjabin.[31]

Ivanov was, however, not only a prolific public lecturer. He was chosen to represent TEO at the First All-Russian Congress on Adult Education in early May, 1919 with a paper on the "organization of creative forces of the popular collective". In the summary, published in *Theater Herald,* Ivanov for once not only prophesied a revival of collective creativity but also proposed concrete action. He admon-

---

[29] *Ibid.,* p. 201–202. Already in 1907 Ivanov had defended the view that Dionysos, through the Thracians, in fact was a god of the Slavs, cf. *Po zvezdam*, p. 234.

[30] Ivanov's activities in TEO is documented in *Sovetskij teatr. Dokumenty i materialy. Russkij sovetskij teatr 1917–1921,* L. 1968, passim.

[31] The detailed reports on the lectures on Tragedy were published in the following issues of *Vestnik Teatra* 1919: No 1 (Feb. 1–2), p. 4, No 3 (Feb. 8–9), p. 4, No 6 (Feb. 15–16), p. 5, No 11 (March 11–13) p. 4. The works of Wagner and Skrjabin were treated in two texts signed by Ivanov, "Zerkalo iskusstv" in *VT* 1919 No 4 (Feb. 10–12) p. 2–3, and "O Vagnere" (a speech held at the Bolshoi Theater), *VT* 1919 No 31–32 (June 9–15), p. 8–9, and in a detailed report on Ivanov's lecture on a Skrjabin evening at the "Red Cock" club in *VT* 1919 No 26 (May 14–16), p. 6.

ished the local powers in the country to 1) support the formation of big choruses all over the country, introducing at the same time elements of action in the chorus; develop the popular festivals along dramatic principles, at the same time encouraging everyone's active participation; 3) arrange outdoor theater performances, mainly such characterized by the "representation of heroic deeds and popular movements and, finally, by the ideal element inherent in the symbolic images of myth, fairytale and legend".[32]

For a moment it would seem as though Ivanov's idea of the synthetic, all-uniting mystery theater was in tune with the times. Revolutionary mass spectacles and pageants were being discussed and prepared by theater groups all over the country. The Proletkul't theoretician Keržencev had published a book, *Tvorčeskij teatr* (*Creative Theater*), which basically was a "proletarization" of certain notions of cultic theater, demanding the abolition of the border between stage and audience as a consequence of the abolition of class differences and individualism in the new society.[33] In spite of his refined symbolism and his mystical-religious philosphy, Ivanov had become an authority often referred to, with or without direct quotation, in the debates in *Theater Herald*. And for once, in the production of Verhaeren's *Les Aubes* in 1920, it seemed as if Mejerchol'd was going to give up his concept of the professional actor confronting and controling his audience in favour of a pseudo-collectivist form with a chorus as a uniting link between stage and audience.[34]

The pantomimes and mass spectacles of the first years of the revolution, usually culminating in the unification of actors and audience in the apotheosis of the victorious people, no doubt corresponded to certain principles of the cultic theater: the synthesis of the arts (drama, music, poetry, art); the transformation of the political content of the play into allegorical forms of mystery play; and the abolition of the dualism between active actors and passive spectators,

---

[32] "K voprosu ob organizacii tvorčeskich sil narodnogo kollektiva v oblasti chudožestvennogo dejstva", *VT* 1919:26 (14–16/5) p. 4.

[33] Cf. Kleberg, " 'People's Theater' and the Revolution", p. 189–191.

[34] In his explanation of the principles of the production of *Les Aubes* at Theater RSFSR–1 in Moscow, inviting the audience to take part in the performance in the "rôle" of the revolutionary people, Mejerchol'd referred to Ivanov as a pioneering critic of the division of stage and audience, cf. V. Mejerchol'd, *Stat'i. Pis'ma. Besedy. Reči*, t. 2, M. 1968, p. 14–16.

the latter functioning as signs in the allegorical play. Ivanov himself, however, never commented on the concrete results of the revolutionary mass theater, although he had given impulses to it at the Congress on Adult Education. Of course it seems hard to imagine the refined symbolist applauding the amateur performances of the early Proletkul't theaters or participating in the carnevalesque pageants on the revolutionary holidays. A "cultic" theater where the religious essence of art, as Ivanov understood it, was replaced by a new, revolutionary mythology could hardly appeal to the poet. There is, however, also a more general reason for Ivanov's reserve towards the practical realization of the principles of cultic theater.

Vjačeslav Ivanov's realm as a theater aesthetic thinker was rather that of the ideal than that of realization, rather the theoretical postulation than criticism. His idea of theater as a mystical "collective happening" was an ideal construction, principally unattainable. In fact, it was only to be found in the Utopias of the distant past or the dim future. In this way Ivanov was a true utopianist: the further he was from the realization of his idea of the cultic theater, the more it gained in brilliance; the closer the idea came to concrete theatrical practice, the less he was excited by the results. In the 1st of May issue, 1920 the symbolist printed his last article in *Theater Herald*.[35] On May 1, the first huge theatricalized manifestation under professional guidance took place in Petrograd, *The Mystery of Freed Labor*. When the wave of revolutionary mysteries and mass spectacles culminated in Soviet Russia, Ivanov had already turned his back on contemporary art and returned to his academic research in the pre-history of Dionysian religion, that is, going even further back into the past than Friedrich Nietzsche once had in search of the sources of tragedy.[36]

Stockholm

---

[35] "Množestvo i ličnost' v dejstve", *VT* 1920: 62 (27/4–2/5), p. 5.
[36] Ivanov defended his doctoral dissertation *Dionis i pradionisijstvo* in 1921 in Baku, where it was printed in 1923.

J. Douglas Clayton

The Play-within-the-play as Metaphor and Metatheatre in Modern Russian Drama

It is the intention in this paper to sketch the role of the play within the play (p.w.p.) and its attendant phenomena metatheatre and quotation in Russian drama/theatre in the period beginning with Čechov and ending with Jurij Oleša's *Spisok blagodejanij* (*The List of Assets*).[1] This study was prompted by the observation that the device was particularly productive precisely during this period in Russia, and that the reasons for this popularity lie in the direction which Russian theatre had taken. There is no literature which focuses on p.w.p. as a feature of Russian drama, although the parallel phenomenon of inserted texts in other, narrative genres has received attention.[2]

Recent Western research has shown that p.w.p. has its roots in the nature of dramatic illusion itself, and has sought to show that it may have central cathartic and generic functions.[3] Viewed structurally, it appears as a form of bracketing, closely allied with metatheatre and quotation, here considered as variants of p.w.p.[4] That the demarca-

[1] Preliminary versions of this paper were read at the international conference of Slavists at Garmisch-Partenkirchen in October 1980 and at the Symposium on Russian Theatre and Literature 1900–1930 in Stockholm in April 1982. The author is grateful to the participants at the latter for many suggestions and improvements which have been incorporated in this text.

[2] See, for example, *Trudy po znakovym sistemam*, 14, Tartu 1981. For a lengthy study of inserted narrative, the reader is referred to Lucien Dällenbach, *Le Récit spéculaire: Essai sur la mise en abyme*, Paris, 1977. A pioneering study of p.w.p as an international phenomenon is to be found in Robert J. Nelson, *Play Within A Play*, New Haven, 1958.

[3] See Alain Michel, "Le Théâtre et l'apparence: d'Euripide à Calderon", *Revue des Sciences Humaines*, 145 (janvier–mars), p. 9–16; and Lionel Abel, *Metatheatre: A New View of Dramatic Form*, New York 1963: "Metatheatre has replaced tragedy", p. 72. Abel was really speaking about *metadrama*, not *metatheatre*, since his analysis is of the literary text, not the theatrical one. Calderwood pushes Abel's notions of metadrama much further than the purview of this study: James Calderwood, *Shakespearean Metadrama*, Minneapolis 1971.

[4] The term is taken from Keir Elam, *The Semiotics of Theatre and Drama*, London 1980, p. 59. From Elam comes, too, my distinction between theatre and drama, and the notation for the "imagined worlds".

tion between these terms is difficult to establish and risks being arbitrary will become apparent in the following discussion. Indeed, it may be taken as a constant in discussions on p.w.p. that each example is to some extent *sui generis* and that the phenomenon is therefore very resistant to classification.

This is not to say, however, that there are not certain generalizations which can be made about p.w.p. The first and most obvious feature is that p.w.p., by definition, is *bracketed,* i.e., *parenthetical.* In *Hamlet,* the play could not begin in the dramatic world of Hamlet the Dane and end in the dramatic world of *The Murther of Gonzago,* for then instead of one play *Hamlet* in which a compositional and plot element is the play-within-the-play, we would have a string of two co-equal plays. It follows, therefore, that the dramatic world of Hamlet (WD) is the dominant illusion, and that the world of Gonzago (Wd) is "read" by the audience as subordinate and factitious. In *Hamlet,* the classical type of p.w.p., the subordinate playlet forms a plot element in the larger play, while retaining its own subordinate reality. A second constant feature of p.w.p. is the fact that there is understood to be a metaphorical relationship between the two texts. This is again clear from the example of *Hamlet* where, in Wd, Gonzago is "read" by the audience and the "audience" (onstage) as Hamlet's father, Baptista as Gertrude, and the murder of Gonzago as a metaphor for the murder of Hamlet's father.

In addition to these constants, we may list a certain number of effects which frequently, though not always, accompany the p.w.p. Firstly, there is the irony which results from the stylistic or other contrast between the two worlds and which serves metatheatrically to parody an acting and/or literary style.[5] Further metatheatrical or metadramatic effects may arise from the foregrounding of theatrical conventions and exposure of theatrical illusion through the embedded text, e.g., Hamlet's reflections on the "deceit" of acting in the speech "O, what a rogue and peasant slave . . ." Paradoxically, the effect of these may be to strengthen the mimetic force of the dominant illusion. Thus, the audience does not make the leap from the deceit of the player who weeps for Hecuba to that of the actor playing

---

[5] Compare Olle Hildebrand's definition of metatheatre: "By metatheatre is meant a theatrical presentation which in some way comments on or questions theatricality itself", *Harlekin Frälsaren. Teater och verklighet i Nikolaj Evreinovs dramatik,* Uppsala 1978, p. 17.

Hamlet himself—on the contrary, it is drawn more deeply into understanding and sympathizing with Hamlet's dilemma. That is to say, the metatheatrical force of p.w.p. need not be directed at the entire institution of the theatre, but merely at one aspect of it.

Another feature of the p.w.p. is that the embedded text is frequently a fragment. This is evidently because of the danger that the subordinate dramatic world (Wd), if pursued too long, may usurp the position of the dominant dramatic world (WD) from which it has temporarily taken over. The problem of the rival claims of both worlds on the credence of the audience is a central one and may take the form of a "battle of illusory worlds" which the dramatist manipulates to his own advantage. Other aspects of this "battle" are the rivalry of the two titles, and also the oscillation of certain characters between characters in WD and "audience" *or* character in Wd.[6]

There are two related phenomena which should be added to the discussion of p.w.p. in the Russian context, namely quotation and metatheatre, whose boundaries with p.w.p. are far from fixed. In the quotation, the embedded "play" is from a text familiar to the audience. The p.w.p., by contrast, is a text composed by the author, albeit with reference to the generic and traditional expectations of the audience. The quotation can be much briefer, like a shorthand, since the world invoked is known. The generalizations about p.w.p. made above apply to it; specifically, its metaphorical and metatheatrical functions are readily apparent in the examples discussed below.

Another question is the relation of p.w.p. to metatheatre itself. Generally speaking, we may say that metatheatre, or theatre in the theatre, is an embryonic form of p.w.p. or, expressed differently, p.w.p. is usually metatheatrical, and metatheatre is frequently in the form of a p.w.p. Metatheatre may be simply a prologue and epilogue, it may go so far as to include its own characters: director, prompter, and "audience" who comment on the action. The world of the theatre (Wt) thus created is not, it should be stressed, coextensive with the actual world of the actors and audience. On the contrary, it "foregrounds" the distance between the two. Metatheatrical characters in Wt may even be involved in a plot, so that metatheatre tends to blend into p.w.p. rather than be rigidly distinguished from it. Perhaps the feature of metatheatre which divides it from p.w.p. proper—apart

---

[6] These subordinate roles are called "secondary theatre" by Hildebrand (*ibid.*).

from the absence of a secondary plot structure—is the fact that it challenges the illusion of the play, but does not seek to replace it with another "dominant" illusion. Metatheatre, then, is subversive and anti-mimetic, and tends to reorient the theatre towards play.

European theatre has seen certain periods of popularity of p.w.p. It was widely used in post-Renaissance England by Kyd, Middleton, Johnson, Massinger and Shakespeare in Elizabethan drama, and by Moliere, Calderon, Cervantes, in French and Spanish Golden-Age theatre.[7] In the eighteenth century Carlo Gozzi and his German follower Ludwig Tieck were inspired by the metatheatre of *commedia dell'arte,* but it was not until the end of the nineteenth century that p.w.p. acquired an importance comparable to that of the post-Renaissance period. In the twentieth century the p.w.p. serves the tendencies in modern art towards self-consciousness, foregrounding of the artistic activity itself, irony, and the rejection of the illusionistic poetics which preceded it.[8]

The earliest example of p.w.p. to be discussed is also one of the most original: Čechov's *Lebedinaja pesnja* (*The Swan Song,* 1887) uses the "quotation" variant. It takes place in an empty theatre from which the "audience" has departed. There is thus, apart from the actual audience and the "audience"—Nikita, a "zero audience" whose absence is eloquent. Svetlovidov reminisces with the aged prompter on his past in the theatre and declaims fragments from various classics: *Boris Godunov, Lear, Hamlet, Othello,* Puškin's poem *Poltava,* and Griboedov's *Gore ot uma* (*Woe from Wit*). Nikita himself is obliged to oscillate between "audience" and character in the fragments from *Lear* and *Hamlet.*

The essential theme of *Lebedinaja pesnja* is the ability of art (even such an ephemeral art as acting) to survive the ravages of time. In the play Svetlovidov's claim—"Where there is talent, Nikita old boy, there is no old age"—triumphs for an instant as he recreates his different roles—despite the neglect of the "audience" and colleagues who had forgotten him even on his benefit night. The thematic

---

[7] See Arthur Brown, "The Play within a Play," *Essays and Studies by Members of the English Association,* XIII (1960), p. 36–48; the essays in "Théâtre dans le théâtre", *Revue des Sciences Humaines,* 145 (janvier–mars 1972), p. 9–142; and Robert Nelson, *op. cit.*

[8] It may also serve directly revolutionary goals. See Reinhold Grimm, "The Play Within a Play in Revolutionary Theatre", *Mosaic,* IX, 1 (Fall 1975), p. 41–52.

concerns of the play are echoed metaphorically in the selection of the passages recited. Thus, the defiance which the old man feels towards his "audience" in general and, in particular, toward the great love of his life who could not reconcile herself to the prospect of marriage to an actor, is reflected in the passages from *Boris Godunov*, *Othello*, and *Hamlet*. It is one of the most exquisite ironies of the play that that "audience" is absent and does not experience that defiance, nor Svetlovidov's last moment of glory, although we, the real audience, do witness it.

The secondary theme in *Lebedinaja pesnja* is the Hamletian one of the falseness of acting. The fact is not lost on us that the first passage quoted is from the false Dmitrij's response to Maria Mniszek. On different planes Otrep'ev's assertion "I am the Carevič" is a literal lie, yet the metaphorical truth, for in Puškin's play he appears as the avenging shade who will make Godunov atone for his bloody murder of the infant Dimitrij. This truth/lie oscillation is the essence of theatre. That is to say, when the actor Svetlovidov states "I am the Carevič" we have another literal lie which is metaphorically true. This metadramatic perception is pursued in the Hamlet passage, in which Svetlovidov/Hamlet taunts Guildenstern/Nikita: to play on the recorder is as easy as lying. Hamlet sees through Guildenstern's "act" and goads him for his lack of talent: to *act,* that is to dissimulate perfectly, is beyond him.

Lebedinaja pesnja is thus structured around different plots—invoked in a few lines, but wholly present in the consciousness of Svetlovidov, Nikita and the audience. The metaphorical application of each quotation is clear, as is its metadramatic function as a comment on theatrical illusion.

P.w.p. also plays an important role in Čechov's *Čajka* (*The Seagull*, 1896). Among other things, this is a play about art itself, specifically the conflict between the symbolist drama of Treplev and the conventional realism of Trigorin. Treplev's playlet is the p.w.p. which forms the main episode in the first act. Čechov gives us a clue as to how to interpret the episode by references to *Hamlet* which form a subtext. Like the "mousetrap", the playlet serves to confront Arkadina and Trigorin—and is therefore a plot episode. It is also a metaphor for the larger drama, for the vision of Treplev's beloved—sitting on a rock and representing the spirit of the world attacked by the glowing eyes of the devil—personifies Treplev's own fears, soon to be realized,

75

about the fate of his idealism (and his love). The playlet itself is a pastiche of Maeterlinckian, "pre-Raphaelite" theatre, yet, by predicting a time when all will be dead, it comments sarcastically on the art of Trigorin and Arkadina which, in Treplev's eyes, is indeed dead.[9]

Aleksandr Blok's *Balagančik* (*The Fairground Booth*), produced by Mejerchol'd in 1906, represents a radical departure from Čechov's theatre. It uses the metatheatrical techniques of the harlequinade to ridicule both the static, death-obsessed theatre of Maeterlinck, represented by the Mystics (who see in the approach of Colombine the onset of death and who understand her braided hair [*kosa*] to mean "scythe"—of death), and also the audience's expectations of a realistic theatre—represented by the intrusions of the "Author", whose "unrealized play" has been usurped by the harlequinade.[10] The name *Balagančik*, an endearing diminutive of *balagan*, often used pejoratively like the English "farce", is programmatic, signalling the bringing to the Russian stage of the styles and conventions of popular theatre, especially the *commedia dell'arte*. In it the conventions of the theatre are foregrounded and become an object of play. Thus the metadramatic content of the play finds its metatheatrical equivalents on the stage, as we see from Rudnickij's description: "The stage was unexpectedly open to its full depth. The wings were hidden with blue canvas, and a blue horizon was suspended at the back, so that an impression of uninterrupted blue space was obtained. This penetrating blue background contrasted sharply with the flimsy white structure of a little theatre which had been constructed on the stage."[11] The artificiality of the *balagan* was further emphasized when, at a crucial point, the entire set was hoisted up out of sight, leaving Pierrot alone onstage.

The mock battle of different concepts of theatre is the central

---

[9] Typical Maeterlinckian elements in the playlet are its static form, the remoteness of the time, the recurrence of such words as "death", "soul", "mourn", and "swamp", reminiscent of Maeterlinck's *Serres chaudes* and the ungainliness of the language, see W.D. Halls, *Maurice Maeterlinck: A Study of his Life and Thought*, Oxford 1960, p. 45).

[10] I use the term "unrealized play" to designate the scenario which the "Author" tries to impose on the *balagančik*—what Harold Segel calls "not a fully-developed play-within-a-play, but the contours of one", *Twentieth-Century Russian Drama: From Gorky to the Present*, New York 1979, p. 125.

[11] K. Rudnickij, *Režisser Mejerchol'd*, Moskva 1969, p. 91.

drama of the play, rather as in *Čajka*. If, in Čechov, the embracing, realist poetic wins, then in Blok's play the subversive poetic takes over the play. In *Čajka* Treplev's play had used the lake as a backdrop. This was perhaps a mocking response by Čechov to the demands for "unnecessary truth" in the theatre (as well as serving other symbolic functions in the play). Actually, of course, that lake was itself a backdrop, another theatrical convention. Thus, the episode in Blok when Harlequin jumps through the backdrop is a response to Čechov's p.w.p. in the same idiom.

After *Balagančik* the metatheatrical possibilities of *commedia dell'arte* were thoroughly explored in the Russian theatre—both in translations and productions of foreign plays (Gozzi's *Turandot* and *Amore delle tre melarance*, Tieck's *Der gestiefelte Kater*, Benavente's *Los intereses creados*) and in plays by Michail Kuzmin, Nikolaj Evreinov, and Vladimir Solov'ev. One may even speak of a Russian variant of *commedia dell'arte,* in which the traditional characters are supplemented by such new metatheatrical figures as the "Author", the "Director", the music conductor, and so on. The most influential figure in this movement was Vsevolod Mejerchol'd, for whom metatheatre was intimately related to the problem of the relationship between stage and audience and the elimination of the proscenium arch.

In the theatre of Nikolaj Evreinov metatheatre and p.w.p. reached a highly developed form. In his early play *Veselaja smert'* the metatheatrical aspects were limited to the prologue, epilogue, and asides addressed by Pierrot to the audience. As Evreinov developed his theories, p.w.p. even acquired a philosphical dimension.[12] Evreinov's most innovative use of p.w.p. is the dress rehearsal of *Quo vadis* in Act Two of *Samoe glavnoe* (*The Main Thing*). The satire is directed at the mediocrity of provincial acting and direction, the squalid text and set. The notion of the p.w.p. as a rehearsal also offers additional comic possibilities, especially through the director, who functions in ways comparable to the "Author" in *Balagančik*. As in Russian variants of *commedia* and in general in p.w.p., the problem of the audience arises: whether to ignore the actual audience, supplant it with a mock one, or "plant" actors among it, as Tieck and

---

[12] See, for example, N. Evreinov, *The Theatre in Life*, New York 1927, p. 202, 240.

Pirandello do. Evreinov solves this by having the director and actors treat the audience as interlopers in the theatre.

The serious ideological content of *Samoe glavnoe,* of which the satire of the p.w.p. is the expression, is voiced by Dr. Fregoli, who proposes to set some of the actors to work in the "Theatre of Life". The third act is devoted to the realization of the theory in another p.w.p. unique to Evreinov, in which the actors become new inmates at a boarding house and assume "roles" in order to make various boarders happier, e.g., to cure a student of his urge to commit suicide. Evreinov's "message" would make the play heavy-handed, except for the humour, which derives from such matters as the actors' slipping out of role. The overlay of play upon play reaches its most intricate in the final act, in which three actors who have been playing different roles in the boarding house now dress up in *commedia dell'arte* masks for Shrove-tide. The transformations of character ("secondary" roles—to use Hildebrand's term) are most complex in the case of the central figure, Paraclete, who likewise appears as Fortune-teller, Dr. Fregoli, Schmidt, a Monk, and Harlequin. The structural complexity of the play, with its overlays of plot, is mirrored in Paraclete's monologue to the audience in which he offers them a variety of possible endings.

The "battle of illusions" implicit in Evreinov's work is echoed in Lev Lunc's *Obezjany idut (The Apes are Coming,* 1923). Here Lunc uses metatheatrical devices derived from *commedia dell'arte*—"improvization", slapstick, audience involvement—to create an absurd, Pirandelloesque comedy. The play is dominated by the Fool, who has a function analogous to that of the play-director in *Samoe glavnoe* or the author in Solov'ev's *Arlekin, pristrastnyj k kartam.* He is the only character who is aware of the audience and, like Blok's "author", tries to impose a scenario on the "chaotic" events onstage. He communicates the title—*Somknutymi rjadami (In Serried Ranks)*—and situation of the unrealized play, of which the only element remaining is a voice off-stage which shouts at intervals: "The enemy is coming."[13] In the unrealized play, which the Fool insists is "revolutionary", a group of people is gathered in a beseiged city during the civil war. The "real" action is more extreme, chaotic, but essentially similar. Hence the distorting-mirror correspondance between "Vrag

[13] Lev Lunc, "Obezjany idut!" *Veselyj al'manach,* Moskva-Peterburg 1923.

idet!"—the cry off-stage—and "Obezjany idut!" ("The apes are coming") of the panic-stricken crowd as they finally organize a defence, tearing up the set to build barricades. Lunc's exploitation of the dramatic potential of metatheatre is at its best in the opening scene, in which several characters enter who "do not know" that they are in a play and are unaware of the dramatic conventions, especially the "fourth wall", so that one of them falls into the orchestra-pit. The exception is the Fool, whom they take for a madman when he indulges in repartee with members of the audience.

Michail Bulgakov's *Bagrovyj ostrov* (*The Crimson Island*, 1928) shows how much the lessons of *commedia* metatheatre had been absorbed by Russian dramatists.[14] The metaplay—a complete theatre in the theatre—frames a play in rehearsal, and is developed into a second plot in the theatre which becomes the dominant illusion to which the inner play relates metaphorically. In the "theatre" plot, apart from such figures as the "Director" and the "Prompter", already familiar, we find a novel character, Savva Lukič, the representative of Glavrepertkom, i.e., the censor. The tension in the play derives from the question of whether he will be persuaded of the play's acceptability and thus ensure the successful career of its "author" Dymogackij (alias Žul' Vern).

The demands of the censor for ideological acceptability are, however, only one of the forces which influence the fate of Dymogackij's play, for equally important is the impact of popular taste which wants colourful farce, slapstick, exotica, and extravagant stage effects. The inner play serves as a parody of these, although it is so long that it must still hold the audience's attention. The contradictory demands of popular taste and ideology become clear when Savva Lukič, who has enjoyed the play, then bans it. The metatheatrical elements—the portrayal of the "author" as an undignified figure of fun whose creation is treated with cavalier disregard, the prompter, the addresses to the audience, all these have their antecedents in Russian dramatic writing, but are infused with a new relevancy because they reflect in farcical form very real problems. The ironies are heightened in the second finale, "improvised" to snatch comedy from

[14] For a thorough study of the p.w.p. in *Bagrovyj ostrov*, see Herta Schmid, "Das Verfahren des Illusionsbruchs in Bulgakovs *Bagrovyj ostrov*," *Canadian-American Slavic Studies*, 15, 2–3 (Summer-Fall 1981), p. 216–237.

the jaws of tragedy by making the play acceptable to Savva Lukič in his official capacity, for it does not escape the perspicacious onlooker that here the allegory (the mutiny of the English soldiers, symbolizing the spread of revolution and the world-wide triumph of the International) parts company with reality.

The metaphorical implications of the inner play are made more complex if we realize that they relate not only to the world in the theatre, but to real life:

Wd: Wt: W

or, expressed in terms of the hero:

Kiri-Kuki: Dymogackij (Žul' Vern): Bulgakov.

In the allegory of the revolution in the inner-play, Kiri-Kuki is the equivalent of Kerenskij.[15] He betrays the "revolution", but, unlike Kerenskij, returns to the crimson island and is forgiven. Thus Dymogackij, the "author" who assumes the role of Kiri-Kuki in the inner play, may be seen as defining Bulgakov's own ideological relationship to the Soviet State. That that relationship is precarious is suggested by the potential tragedy of the ending, which is averted only by last-minute extemporizing by the "director". Also, Dymogackij, in submitting his manuscript, is surrendering his artistic integrity. The "happy ending" which makes the outer play a comedy is achieved by the "mutilation" of the inner play, and Dymogackij's success is material rather than artistic. The p.w.p. thus permits Bulgakov to describe allegorically (and lament) the indignities to which the Soviet dramatist was subjected. The traditional role of the "author" as a comic figure is thus used by Bulgakov for self-directed irony, and has a real existential and political content.

In Bulgakov's Mol'er (Molière, 1930), the p.w.p. elements take the form of quotations in the first and last scenes, which take place backstage at the Palais Royal. The audience has a glimpse through the wings onto the stage, so that it can see Molière acting, and is aware of, but cannot see, the "audience" (cf. Lebedinaja pesnja). The function of the quotations is metaphorical: in the first scene Molière is dressed as Sganarelle (presumably from L'École des maris), which foreshadows the fact that Molière, who has just decided to marry Armande Béjart, will lose her (as Sganarelle does Isabelle). The

---

[15] See Ellendea Proffer's interpretation in her introduction to Michail Bulgakov, The Early Plays of Mikhail Bulgakov, Bloomington 1972, p. 246.

relevance of the last quotation is also clear: Molière, persecuted and ill, is ironically playing Argan from *Le Malade imaginaire*. The grotesque, threatening masks of the examiners who interrogate him correspond to the secret *cabale de dévots* which has been persecuting him. The fragments of the comedies which are incorporated in the play thus serve, paradoxically, to intensify the tragedy of Molière's fate and, by extension, illustrate how closely comedy and tragedy are related for Molière.

Although Majakovskij ridiculed Bulgakov, there is a great deal of similarity between his use of p.w.p. in *Banja* (*The Bathhouse*, 1929) and *Bagrovyj ostrov*. In *Banja* the p.w.p. takes the form of an entire act in which the "director" discusses the play with Pobedonosikov, who is a recalcitrant bureaucrat in the play. There are strong parallels between Majakovskij's Pobedonosikov and Bulgakov's Savva Lukič, the p.w.p. serving a clear polemical purpose in Majakovskij's struggle with Soviet philistinism. Although inserted within the play, the act in the theatre in *Banja* corresponds to the metatheatrical framing in *Bagrovyj ostrov*: in particular the figure of the "director" in each play invites comparison in the way he parodies philistine taste while pandering to it, but, significantly, Majakovskij has no "author" figure.

In Jurij Oleša's play *Spisok blagodejanij* (*The List of Assets*, 1931) a quotation from Hamlet—the "recorders" passage used by Čechov in *Lebedinaja pesnja*—forms the p.w.p. It is read twice in the course of the play—once before a group of Soviet workers, the second time in Paris for Maržeret, the theatrical agent. The double reading of the passage functions in two ways. Firstly, it acts as a kind of epigraph to the drama, inviting us to seek the metaphorical parallels between Lelja's dilemma and that of Hamlet: that is to say, her indecision sets in motion the concatenation of circumstances which destroys her. The struggle for the soul of Lelja—firstly by Fedorov on the Soviet side, then by Tatarov the émigré—parallels the attempts by Guildenstern to penetrate Hamlet's secret.

The function of the "quotation" is thus to serve as a signal to the audience to interpret the play as a sort of pastiche of *Hamlet*. It also serves, however, as a plot episode, the repeated readings corresponding to successive stages in Lelja's internal debate as to the pros and cons of the Soviet regime. For the first reading, Lelja is surrounded by the collective of actors, and has her fellow-actor with her in the role of Guildenstern. Her reading is a challenge thrown down by art to a hostile proletarian audience, a rejection of *dirigisme* in art. The atmosphere of the first reading contrasts with the isolation and vulnerability of Lelja in her second reading before Maržeret, whose indifference to art is revealed when he suggests that she try instead a titillating music-hall number using the recorder. In fact, the recorder assumes the function of a metaphor for art. Neither proletarian audience nor capitalist understands art (for different reasons), just as Guildenstern does not understand how to play the recorder. Only the Chaplinesque unemployed begger can play it, which makes him, in a sense, a kindred spirit to Lelja.

Oleša's is the last important play of this period to use a p.w.p. As we have seen, p.w.p., metatheatre, and quotation are intimately connected with the notion of an anti-mimetic theatre. The shift to Socialist Realism in 1932 therefore brought an end to its usefulness. That it was productive in the early years of this century was to be attributed to the "self-directedness" of modernist art, the experimentalism and breaking of old theatrical forms, and the preoccupation with theatrical convention. In the theatre, as in painting, Harlequin was a revolutionary figure, and the p.w.p. the source of what Wylie Sypher calls the "oscillation of appearances" which he perceives as the essence of Cubist drama. Evreinov and Lunc parallel Pirandello in the way they use the battle of worlds. After the revolution p.w.p. served to highlight the ideological dilemma, and to present to the public the difficulties of conforming to the political requirements of the Soviet State and the shifting tastes of the Soviet theatre-going public.

Ottawa

Harold B. Segel

Russian Cabaret in the European Context: Preliminary Considerations

As we approach the study of the late 19th- and early 20th-century cabaret in Europe as a whole, not just in Russia, certain misconceptions must be confronted immediately.[1] The first is that the cabaret was a marginal cultural activity and not an aspect of the development of the arts to be taken seriously. But the close collaboration of major artists which such cabarets as the "Chat Noir" (Black Cat) in Paris, the "Els Quatre Gats" (Four Cats) in Barcelona, the "Elf Scharfrichter" (Eleven Executioners) in Munich, the "Fledermaus" (Bat) in Vienna, the "Zielony Balonik" (Little Green Balloon) in Cracow, the "Letučaja myš'" (Bat) in Moscow, and "Brodjačaja sobaka" (Stray Dog) in Petersburg, and the "Cabaret Voltaire" in Zurich refutes such an assumption.

Another widespread misconception—more easily rectified— ascribes the very origin of the cabaret, at least in its quintessential or definitive form, to German sources. Predicated on the belief that cabaret was shaped by the social and political tensions of the interwar years, this view identifies the Berlin of the 1920s and early '30s as the seat of the prototypical European cabaret.

What we must finally understand about cabaret is that in its early, most vibrant, most creative period—from its inception in the Parisian "Chat Noir" in 1881 up to and including the birth of Dada at the "Cabaret Voltaire" in 1916—it was no marginal activity but instead a cultural and artistic phenomenon of some significance created by those same factors underlying the great upheaval in the arts in Europe in the late 19th and early 20th centuries. Not only can the appearance of cabaret in the late 19th century be viewed as symptomatic of that ferment, but as a microcosm of a larger pattern of change marked by the breakdown of old forms as a stage in the development of the early

---

[1] For a general account of the cabaret from its beginnings to the present, but minus coverage of Spain and Eastern Europe, see Lisa Appignanesi, *The Cabaret*, New York 1976. My own article, "Fin-de-siècle Cabaret" (*Performing Arts Journal*, Vol. II, No. 1, Spring 1977, pp. 41–57), is a brief survey of the turn-of-the-century cabaret.

20th-century avant-garde, that is of expressionism, futurism, surrealism, and Dada. Moreover, a convincing case can be made, I feel, for the turn-of-the-century cabaret as a kind of proving ground of such change, or what the Russians call a *tvorčeskaja laboratorija,* a creative, experimental laboratory.

If cabaret evolved, mostly after World War I, into a predominantly commercial establishment that is not what it was, or was meant to be, in the beginning. Until commercialization dissipated the elitist artistic aura, cabaret functioned primarily as a wholly or mostly private meeting place of artists eager to come together to entertain one another by reading, performing, or displaying works of an unconventional or experimental nature unconcerned about public acceptance or critical approbation. The common denominator, and a major factor in the very genesis of cabaret, was the dissatisfaction of artists with then predominant modes of artistic expression. In literature and drama this meant, above all, a repudiation of naturalism, on the one hand, and of symbolism, on the other. The discontent, particularly of younger artists, with contemporary social and political forms, their disillusionment with and sense of alienation from the conventions and institutions of the bourgeois 19th century, also affected their attitude toward the Naturalists and the Symbolists. In their social and metaphysical concerns both were regarded as deterministic in outlook and both came to be faulted for placing art at the disposal of social, philosophical, or occult doctrines. Change, it was felt, could come only through rejuvenation, through the recovery of the lost spontaneity, intuitive power, and wonderment of childhood and youth. Art, like society itself, had to be freed from the bonds of conventions, forms, and systems. That this liberation could be achieved, in large measure, through a rediscovery of the element of play was universally recognized. And it was to understand play again and to make play a source of artistic transformation that the late 19th-century artist turned to the sensibility of the child and to the world as well of popular culture. From this redirection of interest and focus came the characteristic enthusiasms of the turn-of-the-century artist: the circus, with its clowns, acrobats, and make-belive, and the fairground with its puppet shows and pantomime. If Frank Wedekind's *Lulu* plays and Leonid Andreev's *Tot, kto polučaet poščečiny (He Who Gets Slapped)* exemplify the impact of the circus milieu on the contemporary drama, how symptomatic of the "discovery" of the world of childhood are such paintings as Henri Rosseau's *Pour fêter le bébé*, depicting a huge overgrown child walking through woods holding a much smaller puppetlike adult by strings, or the Russian poet Michail Kuzmin's "children's songs",[2] among them the well known "Esli zavtra budet solnce" which became the virtual anthem of the Petersburg Bohème whose favorite gathering place was the "Brodjačaja sobaka" cabaret.

As these new attitudes and impulses cohered, so too did the idea of cabaret as an environment compatible by virtue of intimacy and privacy with the elaboration of a new art, a rejuvenated art, unbound by social theory, biology, or metaphysics, neither naturalistic nor symbolistic, indeed irreverently contemptuous of naturalism and symbolism, and motivated by the spirit of play. It was this spirit that Kuzmin captured in the "hymn" he wrote in honor of the "Brodjačaja sobaka":

> Since the birth of the cellar/ Barely a year has elapsed,/ But the "Sobaka" has bound us together/ In a merry-go-round of close friendship./ If your spirit is burdened with care,/ Descend into the depths of the cellar/ And there rest from your woes./ We pull no long faces;/ We're ready ever to drink and sing./ You'll find here singers, ballerinas,/ And artists of all types./ Pantomimes and shows/ Performed with delight...[3]

What enhanced the appeal of the cabaret was the recognition of its suitability as a workshop in which the new art could be forged or, at the very least, as a locus where the advocates of the new could advance their ideas and experiments in an atmosphere of conviviality. For such purposes, no audience was needed, just the fellowship of likeminded artists. When others were permitted entry, they were usually friends of the member artists, and then friends of friends. And even when the cabarets were opened to a wider public, the generally small premises they inhabited in the early period limited the size of an

---

[2] For the best source of information on Kuzmin, including his cabaret activities, see John E. Malmstad, "Mikhail Kuzmin: A Chronicle of His Life and Times", in M. A. Kuzmin, *Sobranie stichov* III, ed. John E. Malmstad and Vladimir Markov, Munich 1977.

[3] The complete text of the Russian poem is in Kuzmin, *Sobranie stichov* I, pp. 455–456.

audience, thus maintaining some semblance of exclusivity as well as close contact between spectator and performer.

The programs of the early cabarets, that is from the "Chat Noir" in Paris to the "Cabaret Voltaire" in Zurich, corroborate the assessment of them as havens for artists hostile to naturalism and symbolism, critical of contemporary society, and attracted to popular culture and the childlike in their search for new means of vision and expression. Generally heterogeneous in nature, the programs ranged from the impromptu, as was often the case with the Petersburg "Brodjačaja sobaka", to the variety theater format encompassing as many as a dozen or more different "numbers" in a single evening. These might include: poetry and prose recitations; songs, whether Parisian *chansons* which were widely admired and imitated[4]—rarely successfully—throughout turn-of-the-century Europe, or ballads recited to musical, usually guitar, accompaniment, like the ones Wedekind performed in his characteristic gritty style at the Munich "Elf Scharfrichter": dances, some traditional and of folk derivation, others inspired by the new uninhibited and barefooted style of Isadora Duncan and her disciples; and theatrical performances in the form of dramatic monologues, sketches, short, generally one-act plays, and puppet and shadow shows. Sometimes longer dramatic works were staged, thus making an entire evening's program or the larger part of a program, but the cabaret style favored short as opposed to longer forms. Full length plays were mounted as a rule by cabarets already evolved into regular albeit small theaters or well on their way to such a transformation, as with the German director Max Reinhardt's "Schall und Rauch" in Berlin, which became the renowned Kleines Theater, or with the Petersburg "Krivoe zerkalo" (Crooked Mirror), especially once the great Russian theater personality Nikolaj Evreinov had assumed its directorship in 1910.

Although performers quickly came to the forefront of cabaret programs, with the limited, and qualified, exception of the Vienna "Fledermaus" and the Petersburg "Brodjačaja sobaka," which retained a strong literary character, the talents of visual artists were prominently in evidence. Architects, painters, and craftsmen either designed the cabarets or decorated their premises, and found addi-

[4] One of the best accounts of the *chanson* in fin-de-siècle Paris is Michel Herbert, *La Chanson à Montmartre,* Paris 1967.

tional outlets for creativity in set and costume design as well as in the construction and painting of marionettes. Furthermore, beginning with the "Chat noir", shadow shows, or "ombres chinoises" (Chinese shadows) as they are called in French, became a popular form of cabaret entertainment which writers and other artists could create together. The texts of the shadow shows, like those of the puppet theater, were the responsibility, of course, of the writers, while the visual artists designed the shadow figures which ranged from sometimes very intricate and sophisticated cardboard cutouts to often elaborate figures or scenes painted on movable glass panels, the latter introduced for the first time at the "Chat Noir" by the artist Henri Rivière. At the Vienna "Fledermaus", Oskar Kokoschka's first theatrical work was a shadow play called *Das getupfte Ei* (The Spotted Egg) for which the artist himself, working with members of the famous Wiener Werkstätte, designed figures of cardboard and copper with movable joints—much in the same primitive-fantastic style as the lithograph illustrations for his macabre poem "Die träumenden Knaben" (The Dreaming Lads) which was also first read at the cabaret.[5] In the Russian context, puppet and shadow shows were performed mostly at the Moscow "Letučaja myš'", which, as its name indicates, was most probably inspired by the Vienna "Fledermaus". They were not offered at the "Krivoe zerkalo" nor did they ever achieve any great prominence at the "Brodjačaja sobaka" or at its successor the "Prival komediantov" (The Comics' Halt), apart from two plays for marionettes written by Kuzmin.

Just how important the visual arts were, in general, for the early cabarets can be judged from the fact that a few of them, such as the "Els Quatre Gats" in Barcelona and the "Zielony Balonik" in Cracow emerged from informal circles of painters. Dominated by artists of considerable Parisian experience such as Santiago Rusiñol, Ramón Casas, Miguel Utrillo, and the young Pablo Picasso, the "Quatre Gats" made its greatest reputation, and contribution, with art exhibitions that established it as the center of turn-of-the-century Catalonian modernism.[6] A similar relationship of cabaret and artistic move-

---

[5] All material on the German and Austrian cabaret in this article is drawn from the Munich and Vienna chapters of this author's book in progress on the late 19th- and early 20-th century European cabaret.

[6] The best account of the "Quatre Gats" in English is Marilyn McCully, *Els Quatre Gats. Art in Barcelona around 1900,* Princeton 1978.

ment existed in Vienna. So active were members of the Vienna Secession and the Wiener Werkstätte in the activities of the "Fledermaus" that the cabaret rightly ought to be viewed as an extension of the Secession and the new Vienna school of applied arts. The interior of the "Fledermaus" was designed mostly by the distinguished Secession architect Josef Hoffmann, while its striking foyer and bar room with their distinctive ceramics were the work of the brilliant Werkstätte artist Berthold Löffler. For artists and designers of the reputations of Gustav Klimt, Kolo Moser, Carl Hollitzer, Oskar Kokoschka, Fritz Zeymer, Jozsef Diveky, and others, collaboration with the "Fledermaus" was nothing out of the ordinary. Much the same can be said for the contemporary Russian cabaret with the distinction that none of the Russian cabarets were as intimately linked with a community of artists in the forefront of the modernist revolution in their respective cultures as were the "Quatre Gats" and the "Fledermaus". Nevertheless, Russian artists as well known at the time as Nikolaj Sapunov, who did the designs for the famous Mejerchol'd production of Blok's play *Balagančik (The Fairground Booth)* in 1907 as well as for several stage works by Kuzmin, Sergej Sudejkin, Aleksandr Jakovlev, and Boris Grigor'ev cooperated closely with the "Letučaja myš'", "Brodjačaja sobaka", and "Prival komediantov". Although the plastic arts were well represented in the Petersburg cabarets, the evolution of the "Letučaja myš'" into a theater of minatures dominated by highly decorative, visually stunning stage pieces necessitated the more active participation of artists, especially Sapunov and Sudejkin, and informed that cabaret with a particular Russian painterliness that attracted great attention wherever it performed.

The restrictive dimensions of the cabarets and the small stages capable of accomodating only a few players at a time were bound to have an impact on the kinds of dramatic performances they could offer. While full-length works were sometimes mounted, as in the case of the annual *szopka* or topical puppet play of the Cracow "Zielony Balonik",[7] most cabarets favored short pieces. The monologues and playlets turned out with such apparent ease by Russian

[7] On the annual *szopka* of the Cracow "Zielony Balonik", see my article "Young Poland, Cracow, and the Little Green Balloon", *The Polish Review,* Vol. V, No. 2, Spring 1960, pp. 74–97. The most thorough Polish account of the "Zielony Balonik" is Tomasz Weiss's *Legenda i prawda Zielonego Balonika,* Cracow 1976.

"miniaturists" of the stamp of N. A. Tëffi and Arkadij Averčenko were typical of the type of drama offered by the cabarets.

But ascribing such scaled down, miniaturized drama primarily to the physical limitations of the average cabaret is to neglect the relationship of the cabaret to the contemporary aesthetic inclination toward small forms. Accompanying the breakdown of the value system of 19th-century bourgeois society was a fragmentation of artistic forms, a retreat, in general, from the grandiose, the pompous, and the formal—a phenomenon observable in the 18th century when, for example, the emergence of a rococo sensibility was symptomatic of a dissolution of classicism that would eventually give rise to a sentimentalist, pre-Romantic movement. The new art of the small of the late 19th and early 20th centuries, or what the Germans refer to as *Kleinkunst*, was an equally noteworthy development, though as yet far less studied. Inquiry into virtually any of the arts of the period offers overwhelming evidence of the movement from the larger to the smaller, but one need go no further than the drama and theater. The phenomenon of the "intimate" or "chamber" theater in Western Europe or of the so called "theater of miniatures" which dotted the Russian urban landscape of the early 20th century arose precisely at this time. If the Litejnyj and Troickij in Petersburg, for example, were typical, no less representative of the same trend was Mejerchol'd's "Dom intermedij" (House of Interludes) and the "Krivoe zerkalo" founded by the actress Zinaida Cholmskaja and her husband the drama critic Aleksandr Kugel' and with which Evreinov was associated from 1910 to 1917. It was Kugel' who once rationalized the cultivation of the new theater of miniatures on the grounds that the "excessive mechanization and overgrowth of theater have so increased that they have inhibited its growth and trivialized it . . . It became necessary, therefore, to fragment the theater into its primary elements, to compress and condense it."[8]

The compression and condensation urged on dramatists by Kugel' was pursued with equal vigor by writers in other genres with the result that the feuilleton and sketch became especially popular. One of the most able of all representatives of this new miniaturized prose style was the archetypical Viennese fin-de-siècle Bohemian Peter Altenberg whose highly concentrated type of sketch, sometimes consisting

[8] Quoted by N. N. Evreinov in *Istorija russkogo teatra*, New York 1955, p. 400.

of only a few lines, seemed the most appropriate style for the wry observations of social behavior which made Altenberg an apparently inexhaustible source of material for the contemporary Vienna cabaret and also a legend in his own time. It was with good reason that Evreinov, for example, included a piece by him in his collection of essays on stage nudity which appeared in Petersburg in 1911 under the title *Nagota na scene* (*Nudity on Stage*). As with dramatic works, the very brevity sought as desirable in prose style among writers who were pointing the way to the avant-garde, such as Chlebnikov, Majakovskij, and Šklovskij in Russia, to mention just a few, favored the cabaret as a suitable place of recitation, one able, moreover, to accomodate a number of works in a single evening. It was not, to repeat, the cabaret that gave rise to the small forms and condensed prose style so popular in the early 20th century, but it seems reasonable to assume that the existence of the cabaret, itself a miniaturized theater, encouraged this type of writing by offering an environment felicitous to it.

The popularity of puppet and shadow shows at the time should also be viewed in the same light. The turn-of-the-century interest in popular culture led to renewed enthusiasm among artists for fairgrounds and their puppet booths. Working on puppet shows became a kind of small scale exercise in the realization of the concept of the *Gesamtkunstwerk* because they involved the skills of writers, artists, and designers. Furthermore, the small size of the dolls, the appearance of usually just a pair of figures on stage at one time, the compressed, simplistic, often repetitive nature of the dialogue, and the considerable amount of physical action enhanced their appeal to the cabarets. Wherever cabaret flourished, therefore, puppet and the related shadow shows were almost always an indispensable part of a program. This was certainly true of the "Letučaja myš'" where dolls came to assume an importance not limited to puppet shows, as we shall soon see. We know, moreover, that the interest in puppetry ran so high in Russia at the time that the Mir Iskusstva group once formed its own puppet theater. Blok's well known little play *Balagančik* typifies this early 20th-century dramatic assimilation of the fairground puppet tradition and could easily have arisen in a cabaret milieu. Even its anti-Maeterlinckian parodic intention was compatible with cabaret theater since so many of the dramatic works staged in cabarets spoofed Materlinck as well as D'Annunzio as the principle exponents of symbolism and neo-romanticism. *Balagančik*, of course, antedates the establishment of the first Russian cabaret, the "Letučaja myš'" (1908), but foreign stimulus ought not to be dismissed out of hand. In some respects, the Blok play resembles Schnitzler's marionette plays, especially *Zum grossen Würstel*, and these did arise in the early years of German-language cabaret where at least one of them, *Der tapfere Kassian*, was staged.[9]

Dramatic presentations figured prominently in most cabaret programs and these tended in turn to be primarily of a satiric and parodic character. Substantiating the earlier point about the anti-Naturalist and anti-Symbolist proclivities of the cabaret is the fact that the satire and parody of cabaret theater was directed principally against Hauptmann, Maeterlinck, D'Annunzio and their followers throughout Europe such as the quasi-Symbolist Andreev in Russia. The overwhelming majority of plays produced by the "Krivoe zerkalo", for example, were parodic and in this respect the Russian cabaret theater replicated a general European pattern. What *distinguished* the "Krivoe zerkalo" was its rapid abandonment of other types of cabaret entertainment in favor of virtual concentration on satiric and parodic drama, reflecting possibly its co-founder Kugel's desire to use the theater as a still more effective weapon in his campaign against Stanislavskij and Mejerchol'd, both of whose philosophies of theater he opposed because of their subordination of actor to regisseur.

With this distinguishing characteristic of the "Krivoe zerkalo" as a point of departure, let us now consider other more specific features of the early Russian cabarets as compared to those elsewhere in Europe. Unlike the emergence of cabaret in other countries, the Russian arose entirely from within a theatrical milieu, to be precise from the tradition of the *kapustnik* or "cabbage party" thrown by actors and actresses of the Moscow Art Theater just before the start of the Lenten period when Russian theaters were traditionally closed. On the initiative principally of an actor of small parts named Nikita Baliev, the *kapustnik* of 1908 became the occasion for the extension of the festivities to other premises and thus it was that the first Russian cabaret was born. It was named "Letučaja myš'" most probably after the Vienna "Fledermaus", which was geographically

---

[9] Virtually all of Schnitzler's works were available in Russian translation by 1909, the year of publication of the final volume of a Russian edition of his complete works.

the closest non-Slavic European cabaret and clearly the most famous at the time in the German-speaking world after the closing of the Munich "Elf Scharfrichter" in 1903.

In its first season and a half, the "Letučaja myš'" adhered to the general cabaret format.[10] But as time went on and more spacious premises were sought to accomodate an ever expanding audience base once the cabaret had become a sensation, the format changed. Variety in the form of songs, dances, recitations, puppet and shadow shows as well as dramatic sketches—while not absolutely abandoned—gave way to programs consisting primarily of theatrical pieces in which decorativeness and visual appeal were the outstanding characteristics. The repertoire was drawn partly from Russian classical literature (Puškin, Gogol', Turgenev, Čechov, and others)—specially adapted, of course, for presentation by the "Letučaja mys'"—and partly from a stock of arrangements of greater visual than literary appeal devised specifically for the cabaret. Of this latter group, the most popular, for which the "Letučaja myš'" became especially renowned, were the "living doll" numbers, some based on Russian folk tradition and popular culture, such as the *lubok*, or cheap print, others of a more cosmopolitan character in which novelty of conception and high stylization, particularly with regard to costumes, were major sources of appeal. Reflecting the contemporary rediscovery of the marionette by the serious artist as well as the theme of the animation of the inanimate in which the fin-de-siècle took such a particular interest, the "living doll" numbers of the "Letučaja myš'" featured actors and actresses who assumed the roles of inanimate dolls—figures in paintings, statues, characters in a *lubok* scene, for example—who come to life at a certain point, dance, sing, recite dialogue in verse or prose, and then at the end of the number return to their original lifeless state. The affinities with Stravinskij's *Petrouchka*, of course, come to mind, but rather than think in terms of influence, it is far more productive to isolate the common source or sources of closely related phenomena.

If the "Letučaja myš'" evolved into a miniature theater prized above all for its colorful "living doll" productions, the "Krivoe zerka-

---

[10] On the "Letučaja myš'", see N. E. Efros, *Teatr "Letučaja myš'" N. F. Balieva*, M. 1918, and L. Tichvinskaja, "Letučaja myš'", *Teatr* 1982, No. 3, pp. 102–112. There is also material on it, and on other Russian cabarets, in Angelo Maria Ripellino, *Il trucco e l'anima*, Torino 1965, pp. 191–210.

lo" in Petersburg, also founded in 1908, took another direction, that of a full-fledged if miniature theater in which drama reigned supreme. Like the "Letučaja myš'", however, the "Krivoe zerkalo" also found its own distinct identity in relation to prevailing European cabaret patterns. Even before Evreinov's seven year directorship, but especially in the period of his hegemony there, the "Krivoe zerkalo" became celebrated for its satiric and especially parodic drama. In this respect it typified the prominence of the parodic element in cabaret art everywhere and the subversive function of this parody with respect to established 19th-century dramatic and theatrical traditions. What set the "Krivoe zerkalo" apart from other cabarets, however, was its institutionalization of cabaret parody as theater, and its concentration on such specific Russian targets as the imperial theater system as "establishment", traditionalist theater, the Moscow Art Theater whose painstaking exaggerated realism made it an easy victim of "Krivoe zerkalo" parody, and the general line of Mejerchol'd's development as a regisseur-dominant as opposed to actor-dominant theorist and practitioner.

Some of Evreinov's major dramatic writing lends itself to interpretation from the perspective of cabaret and "Krivoe zerkalo" parodic orientation.[12] Like Blok's *Balagančik*, Evreinov's personal favorite among his short plays, *Veselaja smert'* (*A Merry Death*), can be seen as echoing the anti-Maeterlinckian satires and parodies of the cabarets in the repudiation of Maeterlinck's morbid fixation on death in favor of an affirmative philosophy of life unafraid of death. Evreinov's best known and most widely performed full length play, *Samoe glavnoe* (*The Chief Thing*), also incorporates a hilarious parody of a typical threadbare Russian provincial theater of the time in virtually the whole of its second act.

Even Evreinov's experiments with monodrama, in particular his most successful *V kulisach duši* (*Behind the Curtains of the Soul*), which was staged at the "Krivoe zerkalo", can be related to a cabaret environment, both in its content and structure. The play's parody of

---

[11] On the "Krivoe zerkalo", see especially Evgenij Kuznecov, *Iz prošlogo russkoj èstrady*, M. 1958, pp. 293–309. There is also good material in D. Zolotnickij, *Zori teatral'nogo oktjabrja*, L. 1976, pp. 156–220.

[12] A fine recent analysis of Evreinov's dramatic work in the light of his theatrical theories is Olle Hildebrand, *Harlekin Frälsaren. Teater och verklighet i Nikolaj Evreinovs dramatik*, Uppsala 1978.

93

Freudian psychology accords wholly with the mocking impulse of the early cabaret in general, while the play's brevity, introductory monologue, spare dialogue, interpolated song, dance, and musical accompaniment, slapstick physical action, and on stage transformation of Songstress No. 2, with its grotesque aspect, represent typical features of cabaret theater. The temptation also exists to posit cabaret influence—at least on some level—for Evreinov's concept of monodrama as a type of play in which the author dramatizes only the inne. states and subjective perceptions of a single individual. That the concept was stimulated in part by Symbolist drama, particularly Maeterlinck, and in part by Freudian psychology—despite the mockery of it in *V kulisach duši*—seems certain. But perhaps a role in the formulation of the concept can also be found for the cabaret with its accomodation of miniaturized drama—and monodrama cannot be sustained for any length of time, as Evreinov discovered with his largely unsuccessful *Predstavlenie ljubvi (The Theater of Love)*—its reduced *dramatis personae*, its embrace of monologue, and the very intimacy of cabaret theater which facilitated the acceptance of a species of experimental drama predicated on the audience's willingness to accept the actions transpiring on stage as the externalization of an individual's psychic states. More important than its possible influence on the concept of monodrama was the cabaret's suitability as a laboratory in which just such experiments in new dramatic form could be staged before audiences for the most part sympathetic to innovation. This was indeed the case with Kokoschka's earliest theatrical works which initiated an Expressionist drama and were first performed in the Vienna "Fledermaus".

With respect to what one writer on Evreinov calls his "polydrama"[13]—meaning a type of drama, related to monodrama, in which the focus is now a single reality viewed from several different perspectives—this may be regarded as a contribution of the "Krivoe zerkalo", or of Evreinov personally, in less original terms. By polydrama in the context of "Krivoe zerkalo" theater, one is meant to understand such works as Boris Gejer's *Évolucija teatra (The Development of Theater)* and Evreinov's *Revizor: režisserskaja buffonada (The Inspector General: a Director's Buffonade)*, both parodies of

[13] Christopher Collins, tr. and ed., *Theater as Life: Evreinov. Five Modern Plays*, Ann Arbor 1973, p. xvii.

specific theatrical styles and of specific Russian playwrights, above all Andreev who as a target of cabaret parody and satire fulfilled a role roughly analogous to that of D'Annunzio in the West.[14] Although the Gejer and Evreinov parodies address *Russian* theatrical phenomena, this type of parodic "polydrama" had already been established in German cabaret theater a few years earlier, particularly by Max Reinhardt. *Karle*, a "Diebskomödie", written by Max Reinhardt, Friedrich Kayssler, and Martin Zickel in 1901, is the second part of a parodic trilogy entitled *Don Carlos an der Jahrhundertwende* in which the authors recast Schiller's classic as they imagine it would be staged by Maeterlinck and Hauptmann. In *Nora*, which Rudolf Bernauer staged at the Berlin cabaret "Die bösen Buben" in 1903, the last scene of the last act of Ibsen's *Doll House* is presented in the different conceptions of, among others, Frank Wedekind, Maurice Maeterlinck, and the Kaiser Wilhelm II's favorite dramatist, Joseph Lauff.

For those familiar with the rarified literary ambience of the famous "Brodjačaja sobaka" it might seem that at least one major Russian cabaret had succeeded in resisting the theatrical imperative of Russian cabaret life generally.[15] If we speak of the "Brodjačaja sobaka" of 1913 and 1914, the impression is essentially correct. By the time of its closure by the police in 1915, the "Sobaka" had become a literary haunt, frequented by Gumilëv, Achmatova, Kuzmin, Majakovskij, Pjast, the close friend and biographer of the poet Blok, Georgij Ivanov, Mandel'štam, Benedikt Livšic, Chlebnikov, and others. Lectures on literature and language as well as poetry readings were frequent—Viktor Šklovskij spoke on "The Place of Futurism in the History of the Language" while Chlebnikov declaimed Futurist poetry there. If the "Sobaka" was not the birthplace either of futurism or acmeism, it played host to the most prominent exponents of both and while on the whole less sympathetic to the Futurists nevertheless provided them with a forum for their poetry and theory. The style of the "Sobaka" was both eclectic and impromptu—there was a great

---

[14] For a general survey of 19th- and 20th-century Russian theatrical parody, see Mark Poljakov's introduction (pp. 6—38) to the anthology *Russkaja teatral'naja parodija XIX načala XX veka*, M. 1976.

[15] On the "Brodjačaja sobaka" and the "Prival komediantov", see Vladimir Pjast, *Vstreči*, M. 1929, pp. 245—299; A. A. Mgebrov, *Žizn v teatre*, Vol. II, M.-L. 1932, pp. 157-189; Georgij Ivanov, *Peterburgskie zimy*, New York 1952, pp. 70—76; Benedikt Livšic, *Polutoraglazyj strelec*, New York 1978, pp. 156—157, 174—191.

deal of spur-of-the-moment recitation and argumentation, but there were also special, more structured evenings such as the one devoted to the great Russian ballerina Tamara Karsavina,[16] and special weeks, such as those in honor of the founder of Italian futurism, Filippo Tommasso Marinetti, the French balladeer Paul Fort, and the immensely popular French comic actor known best under the assumed name of Max Linder,[17] all of whom visited Petersburg and the "Brodjačaja sobaka".

By 1914, and until its closing in 1915, the "Sobaka" was a type of semi-public salon, the favorite gathering place of the Petersburg literary and artistic elite yet open to people from other walks of life all of whom were categorized by Boris Pronin, its founder and master of ceremonies, as *farmacevty* (pharmacists) to distinguish them from the artists who clustered there. At its founding, however, the "Sobaka" was the realization of the so called "Artistic Society of the Intimate Theater" (*Chudožestvennoe obščestvo intimnogo teatra*) whose charter members included the theater people Mejerchol'd, Evreinov, and Fëdor Komissarževskij; the artists Sapunov and Sudejkin; the poet Kuzmin; the writer Remizov; and the composers and musicians Il'ja Sac, Val'ter Nuvel' of the Mir Iskusstva circle, and the music critic Al'fred Nurok.

To better understand Mejerchol'd's part in the establishment of the "Brodjačaja sobaka" and his active role in the first two years there, a look at chronology is useful. Mejerchol'd's own cabaret theater, "Dom intermedij", which he had launched with Kuzmin and Sapunov, had lasted but a year from 1910 to 1911, the same short life span as Evreinov's "Vesëlyj teatr dlja požilych detej" ("Merry Theater for Elderly Children"). When Evreinov was offered the directorship of the "Krivoe zerkalo" in 1910, the opportunity to work with a theater of small forms of greater potential negated the value of the "Vesëlyj teatr" and that enterprise became moribund.

The closing of the "Dom intermedij", however, left Mejerchol'd with no similar outlet and his enthusiasm as Dr. Dapertutto for the experimental possibilities of cabaret theater were too great at the time to remain long ungratified. The solution came in the context of

[16] Karsavina describes the event in her book of reminiscences, *Theatre Street,* New York, 1961, pp. 254–255.

[17] There is a photo of Max Linder arriving in Petersburg on a visit in *Sinij žurnal,* November 29, 1913, No. 48, p. 13.

his friendship with Boris Pronin whose enterpreneurial eagerness to establish his own cabaret or intimate theater was matched by Mejerchol'd's desire to secure a laboratory for the experiments of Dr. Dapertutto. What resulted was the "Obščestvo intimnogo teatra" whose premises in the cellar of the old Daškov mansion on the corner of Ital'janskaja Street and the Michajlovskij Square became known as the "Brodjačaja sobaka" which opened its doors with great fanfare and success on the last day of the year 1911. That Mejerchol'd was the moving spirit behind the "Obščestvo" can be seen from the central importance in the new cabaret's programs of theatrical activities. Moreover, Pronin's desire originally to establish a serious "theater of masks and Colombines"—another temple of the *commedia dell'arte* and pantomime which had figured so prominently in Dr. Dapertutto's theatrical experimentation in 1909, 1910, and 1911—clearly reflected Mejerchol'd's own infectious enthusiasm.

The predominance of theatrical programs, among them a Nativity puppet play by Kuzmin[18], did not compromise the cabaret's exclusivity and informality. Only artists, musicians, and writers, and their friends were admitted and once inside had to provide their own service from a buffet. But as the "Sobaka" evolved into a gathering place for the Petersburg Bohème and gawking outsiders were permitted entry only on payment of an outlandish admission fee collected personally by Pronin at the entrance, the theatrical emphasis receded and literary evenings became increasingly more frequent. The turning point may have been the love suicide of the poet Vsevolod Knjazev, Kuzmin's former lover and an ardent and jealous suitor of Sudejkin's beautiful and talented wife O'lga Glebova—the basis, as we know, of Achmatova's long *Poèma bez geroja* (*Poem without a Hero*). Although he continued to participate in programs after the incident, Kuzmin, who had been extremely active in virtually all aspects of the "Sobaka" previously, sharply limited his association with the cabaret after 1913.

The establishment of the "Prival komediantov" in 1916 after the closing of the "Brodjačaja sobaka" followed the pattern of the latter's founding in terms of Mejerchol'd's involvement and the cabaret's theatrical emphasis.

---

[18] There is an enthusiastic description of the performance of Kuzmin's "vertep kukol'nyj" by Sergej Auslender in *Apollon*, February 1913, no. 2, pp. 66–67.

The first glimmer of the appearance of a successor to the "Sobaka" came in an announcement in the second issue of the journal *Apollon* for 1916 that a new cellar theater named "Zvezdočët" would open in late March of that year with a fresh production of Schnitzler's panto-mime *Der Schleier der Pierrette* (*Šarf Kolombiny*, in Russian), directed by Dr. Dapertutto with sets and costumes by Sudejkin. Again uniting the talents of Mejerchol'd and Pronin, the original plan called for a "Teatr podzemnych klassikov" (Theater of Underground Classics) whose repertoire would include plays by Tieck, Strindberg, Maeterlinck, Claudel, Kuzmin, the Russian authority on the Italian *commedia dell'arte* Konstantin Miklaševskij, and others. With the production of the Schnitzler pantomime in April 1916, which re-ceived only lukewarm reviews, Mejerchol'd's collaboration with the enterprise promptly ceased. The old official designation, carried over from "Sobaka" days, of the "Obščestvo intimnogo teatra" remained, but the cabaret now headed by Evreinov and N. V. Petrov, a young director at the Aleksandrinskij Theater, bore the name of "Prival komediantov".[19] Although its premises were larger and more ornate and its atmosphere more restrained and commercial, the "Sobaka's" successor adhered to a primarily theatrical program. But like the reborn "Krivoe zerkalo" of 1922, which closed its doors forever in 1933, it found the postrevolutionary environment of Soviet Russia less hospitable to the spirit that had reigned earlier and shut down in 1919. The continued existence of a "Krivoe zerkalo" and attempts to preserve a cabaret-like art notwithstanding, the brilliant era of the early 20th-century Russian cabaret—the period from 1908 to 1919— was over. The emigration of Nikita Baliev together with other mem-bers of the "Letučaja myš'" and the reestablishment of the first Russian cabaret in Paris in 1920 as the "Chauve Souris" patently symbolized the end of that era.

Writing of what he regarded as the failure of Russian society to preserve an authentic artistic cabaret, free from commercialization and the presence of the bourgeois, the actor Mgebrov spoke of Russia's lack of culture:

> Russia still lacked sufficient culture to create something similar to Montmartre. Pharmacists and burghers, the bourgeois and

[19] An announcement in the newspaper *Reč'* for Wednesday, April 20, 1916 (Nr. 107, p. 5) gives April 18 as the date of the official opening of the "Prival komediantov".

predators, of whom there have always been and still are so many in our country, indeed had a great idea—the unification of artists of all branches. But they very quickly destroyed the idea and the artists themselves with it. And that is why for me the "Brodjačaja sobaka" in later years almost ceased to exist.[20]

Had he been able to see the development of the cabaret in Europe as a whole in the late 19th and early 20th centuries, Mgebrov's view would doubtless have been more benign because the commercialization he decried with respect to the Russian cabaret was the inevitable fate of cabaret virtually throughout Europe. The intensity with which the spirit of cabaret was entered into, above all by by the participating artists, in the early history of the phenomenon, made it all but impossible to sustain the momentum for long periods of time, hence the frequent closings and openings of cabarets. And even if this were not the case, one can only speculate on how long it might have been possible to preserve the artistic "purity" and integrity of the cabarets without the eventual admission of a paying public in view of the costs of even modest productions and the notorious business sense of so many of the cabaret artists.

What stands out so strikingly in the case of the Russian cabaret in the decade 1908 to 1918 is not so much the capitulation to the bourgeois as the inability of the Russians to develop a cabaret in the archetypical Western sense for any but the briefest period. The reactionary nature of the state and the ever present police surveillance made the kind of social and political criticism typical of the Western cabaret difficult if not completely impossible, denying the Russians, therefore, an important dimension of cabaret art common in the West. There were also specific forms resistant to transplantation in Russian soil, above all the Parisian *chanson* or the type of corrosive, macabre songs for which Wedekind was renowned in Munich in the early years of the century and which had a great influence on the young Bertolt Brecht. The Russian cabaret, in fact, produced no singers or poets with a distinct cabaret identification, in yet another departure from Western experience. What remained was theater and theatrical spectacle, on the one hand, and the heated atmosphere of conflicting avant-garde literary groups, on the other,

[20] Mgebrov, *op. cit.*, pp. 188—189.

and it was from these two sources principally that the Russian cabarets drew their greatest inspiration and sustenance. The predominance of theater in the cabarets was understandable in light of the great ferment in Russian theatrical culture of the time and the virtual impossibility of innovating and experimenting within the world of the imperial theater system. When a great new theater came into being in the late 19th century, the Moscow Art Theater, the style for which it became world famous was regarded as an anachronism by the avant-garde and they turned on it with the kind of disdain reserved previously for the old imperial theaters. Against this background, the overwhelming preoccupation with theater on the part of the authors of cabaret satires and parodies becomes wholly understandable. If we find it proper to speak of a theatricalization of Russian life in the early 20th century, a theatricalization by which the community of artists and intellectuals responded to the greater social and political unreality around them, then Russian cabaret of the early 20th century deserves consideration as another aspect of that theatricalization, of that making life a carnival before the imminent descent into the abyss.

New York

Håkan Lövgren

Sergej Radlov's Electric Baton: The "Futurization" of Russian Theater

Filippo Marinetti's *Variety Theater Manifesto* from 1913 and the 1915 Futurist *Synthetic Theater Manifesto* introduced and anticipated a great number of the elements and approaches which were to abound in the different Russian *avant-garde* theaters in the years immediately following the October Revolution. The Italian Futurists' preoccupation with tangible and crude effects on the spectator, with synthetic and elliptic approaches to theatrical form in order to gain a maximum of dynamism, with the actor as mechanism rather than mind, with the entire performance as a veritable clockwork cranked up to cover the normal five acts in two minutes instead of two hours, were all more or less basic ingredients in the later *avant-garde* efforts of directors like Jurij Annenkov, Sergej Radlov, Kozincev and Trauberg of the FÈKS group, and Sergej Ėjzenštejn.

My intention here however is not to try to prove or insist on a direct and unadulterated line of influence from Italien Futurism to the Russian *avant-garde* theater, but rather to point to conceptual convergences between the two in the development of these directors' performances, particularily those of Sergej Radlov. My hypothesis is that many post-revolutionary Russian *avant-garde* performances were predisposed to dissolve into their constituent elements, i.e. into the forms of popular entertainment (music hall, circus, film) they attempted to adopt and integrate, by weight of the theories and methods they sought to implement and practice. The popular and agitational ambitions of the *avant-garde* theater were accompanied by strongly anti-literary sentiments which led to a close to complete abandonment of dramatic texts and speech. The heavy emphasis on the visual side of the performance, the notion of the "autocratic" director, and the tendency to view the theatrical process in abstract terms of space, time and dynamism, in my opinion, pushed the theater towards the "electric muse"—film—since the cinematic medium promised to give these considerations and categories greater opportunities for artistic realization.

"We are deeply disgusted with the contemporary theater", wrote Marinetti in his manifesto on the Variety Theater[1], "because it vacillates stupidly between historical reconstruction . . . and photographic reproduction of our daily life; a finicking [sic], slow, analytic, and diluted theater worthy, all in all, of the age of the oil lamp" (Marinetti 1972 p. 116). The new era of electricity and urban dynamism demanded a new theater on a par with the swift movement, rapid pace and effectiveness of the machine as seen and interpreted by the Italian Futurists. As the supreme model for this theater Marinetti proposed the Variety Theater, because it is, as he said, "born as we are from electricity, is lucky in having no tradition, no masters, no dogma, and it is fed by swift actuality" (ibid.).

What attracted Marinetti to the Variety Theater was, above all, its alogical nature, the fact that it did not attempt to create the illusion of meaning, of signifying something other than its own immediate being and acting, as Michael Kirby points out in *Futurist Performance*:

> The acrobat and the juggler do not aid in the development of a narrative or pretend to be anywhere other than where they really are. Nor do they generally embody abstract ideas or concepts: the trapeze artiste flies without representing flight. The actions of such variety performers are not symbolic but complete and self-sufficient. The immediate presence of a physical activity or action is enough to create a rewarding experience for the spectator (Kirby 1971 p. 22).

The psychological and metaphysical innocence or indifference of this theater held the promise of a clean break with earlier (Realist and Symbolist) traditions, and its dynamic character offered the possibility of infusing the stuffy theatrical institutions with a breath of fresh and pure theatricality.

---

[1] Some of the Italian Futurist manifestos, among them Marinetti's "The Variety Theater Manifesto" (*Mjuzik-Choll*), were translated into Russian by Vadim Šeršensevič and published in 1914. Cf. *Manifesty ital'janskogo futurizma*, pp. 71–77.

In 1914 Marinetti visited Russia. In Petersburg he honored Mejer-chol'd's Doctor Dapertutto Studio with his presence. An ex-perimental group of actors, the Grotesque Group, had just com-pleted a performance of *Anthony and Cleopatra* when Marinetti suggested they do an improvisation on the theme of *Othello*. "After a three-minute discussion of the tragedy's salient features, the group performed a three-minute résumé of it", Mejerchol'd noted laconi-cally in his journal *The Love of Three Oranges* (*Mejerchol'd 1969* p. 146).[2]

In his 1912 essay "The Fairground Booth" Mejerchol'd had argued for a revival of the improvised theater and the art of the ambulating actor. It was in the technical skill of this actor that the true art of acting and the fundamental laws of theatricality could be found. The emphasis on theatricality and the technical ability of the actor, which Mejerchol'd had hoped would cure the theater of the Realist virus and its servile relationship to literature generally, acquired a definite bias in favor of the circus around the time of the October Revolution. In August, 1917, Mejerchol'd declared in an article called "Long Live the Juggler!": "If I were asked what kinds of entertainment our people need now ... I would say without reflecting: those which only the circus artists are able to give with their art. The people need the kind of art that is capable of infecting the participants by its example of utmost bravery" (Zolotnickij 1976 p. 222).

Two years later Mejerchol'd's declaration became the pretext for one of the first attempts at integrating or introducing popular forms of spectacles, especially the circus, into traditional comedy. Jurij Annenkov, an artist and set designer who had worked with Evreinov[3]

[2] In 1921 Mejerchol'd made this evaluation of Marinetti: "Despite this Futurist scandalmonger's flippant use of the paradoxical, one can understand the hidden meaning behind his anger, his revolt against the theater of halftones, castrated Luther-anism, the temple with its draperies and flacid psychological mysticism, which makes any unaffected spectator feel sick". (Mejerchol'd 1968, 2, p. 29).

[3] Nikolaj Evreinov's experimental performances and extensive theoretical output during the early decades of this century undoubtedly influenced directors like Annen-kov and Radlov. His metatheatrical and reconstructive performances (*Starinnyj teatr*) call to mind Radlov's later efforts in the same direction, but his utopian notion of a theater of play-acting and games appears ultimately more akin to Symbolist esthetic and philosophic ideas than to the concepts of theatrical productivity, plot and theme-less plays, etc. employed by these *avant-garde* directors. In the summer of 1920, Annenkov, Radlov and Evreinov were all involved in organizing mass spectacles in Petrograd. For an excellent account of Evreinov's work, see Hildebrand, 1978

among others, then produced an eccentric version of Lev Tolstoj's *The Fist Distiller* in which a Vertical Devil, a Jester of the Elder Devil, accordion players, acrobats and other circus artists provided amplification of the play's allegorical theme. Whether this "heroic theater", as Annenkov called it, owed more to the interludes in medieval mystery plays[4] than to the Variety Theater might be difficult to determine. At any rate the tenth point of Marinetti's manifesto reads: "The Variety Theater is a school of heroism in the difficulty of setting records and conquering resistance, and it creates on the stage the strong, sane atmosphere of danger" (Marinetti 1972 p. 118).

Danger and heroism would be the fundamental criteria of the future actor's art, according to Annenkov. In connection with his circus approach (*cirkizacija*) in *The First Distiller* he wrote:

> The art of the actor . . . and the degree of perfection he reaches in his profession, are always relative. The art of the circus performer is perfect because it is absolute. If an acrobat makes the slightest miscalculation, if he has a second's weakness, he loses his balance, falls off his trapeze, his act is a failure, he is no longer an artist. The revolutionaries of the theater will find in the circus performer and his self-mastery the seeds of a new form of theater, of the new style (Bablet 1966 p. 112).

Viktor Šklovskij, who seems to have attended most of the wildly experimental theater performances at this time, was fairly impressed by Annenkov's syncretic approach to Tolstoj's morality play. In a comparison between the methods of Annenkov and his successor of sorts, Sergej Radlov, Šklovskij maintained that Annenkov's production remained a unit, despite his introducing characters who were totally unrelated to the story. Annenkov had chosen an already existing play with a strong, basic plot (*sjužet*) and avoided assigning his circus characters any other dramatic function than that which could be inferred from their individual stunts. Radlov, on the other hand, "surrounds his stunts with a poorly developed story line lacking almost any structuring core" (Šklovskij 1923 p. 135). Šklovskij may

---

[4] Cf. Šklovskij's remarks in "The Adorned Tolstoj": "Sometimes however they [the theatrical embelishments] are presented according to the interlude principle, i.e. introduced as distinctive insertions and concentrated on the roles of the jesters or wits, who are not participating in the basic (if such a thing exists) action of the production" (Šklovskij 1923 p. 129).

have exaggerated the coherence of Annenkov's adaptation and the differences between the two directors' approaches to original dramatic material. Both Annenkov and Radlov insisted on great independence in relation to the dramatic text and treated the play as a scenario upon which they could base their experiments.

3.

Sergej Radlov belonged to the pre-revolutionary generation of Mejerchol'd's students. He had been a regular participant in Doctor Dapertutto's Studio and contributor to the journal *The Love of Three Oranges* from 1913 until the dissolution of the studio in 1917. In June, 1918, he formed a theater group called The First Communal Troupe with former members of the Mejerchol'd studio and circus artists. The group continued the search for an improvisational theater begun in the studio and Radlov presented two basic principles for the work of his "popular theater": first, the "theatrical traditionalism" and secondly, the "actor's verbal improvisation" (*Istorija sovetskogo teatra* p. 196).

The principle of "theatrical traditionalism" was meant to bring about the immediacy of the so-called primitive, popular work of art, the ideal of which Radlov associated with the clowning of the circus artist. In that context the meaning of the "actor's verbal improvisation" becomes self-evident—a principle of freedom in relation to the text of any chosen play. It was the Southern European 17th century theater, the Italian improvised mask theater in particular, that Radlov had in mind when he spoke of "theatrical traditionalism". But classical Roman comedies were also included in the popular repertoire. Radlov held the comedy to be the most democratic of theatrical genres because it sought direct communication with the audience, an impulse that had been driven out of the theater during the reign of Realism and Symbolism, and which now only remained alive in the circus arena. In the summer of 1918 Radlov produced Plautus' *The Twins*. The performance seems to have been built around the amplification of the play's dynamic and grotesque features in combination with an extremely pious, restorationist approach to the historic details in costumes and setting. Plautus' gallery of types was portrayed by actors wearing masks which were so carefully reconstructed that the performance received enthusiastic reviews in a journal dedicated to classical antiquity.[5]

4.

In January, 1920, Radlov and Vladimir Solov'ev founded the Theater of Artistic Music Hall Entertainment, which soon after became the Theater of Popular Comedy or simply the Popular Comedy. For the first months it provided performances by Radlov's earlier "circus comedy" group including jugglers, ventriloquists, "Roman gladiators", musical duets and dance numbers by members of the Ballet Academy. Agit plays and social satire soon entered the repertoire and for the May 1st celebrations, 1920, the group prepared a political satire called *The Capitalists' Intrigues* (*Proiski kapitalistov*) in which Radlov presented an arsenal of stock characters in the tradition of the Italian mask comedy.

The idea of the "improvised theater" was the conceptual cornerstone on all levels of Radlov's productions with the Popular Comedy. The performance originated in a scenario written by the author-director, and took shape in the actors' elaboration of any implicit dialogue or monologue, all in accordance with the principle of the "actor's verbal improvisation". Radlov's ambition was to completely do away with the written drama[6] and eliminate those noxious creatures—the professional dramatists—who, hiding in the silence of their rooms, write "verbal ballets" for the directors and actors willing to dance to their tunes.[7]

[5] Cf. S. Cybulskij, "Menechmy" Plavta na scene Zimnego Vodevilja v Narodnom dome v Petrograde", *Germes*, No 22, 1918 Jan-July, pp. 117–118. Quoted in Zolotnickij, 1976 p. 240.

[6] In his "Theater as Production" (*Teatr, kak proizvodtvo*) Arvatov proposed to liquidate the plot/theme in the transitional phase toward the proletarian theater in which the "theatrical action becomes its own theme". Arvatov was favourably inclined towards Radlov, "whose experiments, despite their undeniable dependence on esthetics, are of great symptomatic importance", *O teatre,* Tver', 1922, p. 117, 119.

[7] Cf. *Istorija sovetskogo teatra,* p. 201.

Some of Radlov's "circus comedies" had included film sequences. This was nothing new or original, as Marinetti's manifesto indicates: "The Variety Theater is unique today in its use of the cinema, which enriches it with an incalculable number of visions and otherwise unrealizable spectacles (battles, riots, horse races, automobile and airplane meets, trips, voyages, depths of the city, the countryside the oceans and skies)" (Marinetti 1972 p. 116). What these "otherwise unrealizable spectacles" meant in the context of Radlov's theater becomes clear if we consider the play produced by the Popular Comedy in August, 1920.

The Comedy's performances had been criticized by the advocate of "pure theatricality", Jurij Annenkov, for making concessions to "narrative logics". As a response to this no doubt unwarranted criticism Radlov wrote and produced *The Foster-Child* (*Priemyš*[8]), a Futurist thriller and action drama based on the model of dime store detective novels with all the ingredients Marinetti could ever have wished for.

The Foster-Child centers around the attempts to capture a thief who has stolen documents of great importance to the Soviets. The chase begins among the tables in a restaurant and continues out into the street. The role of the thief is played by the gymnast Serž, who escapes by jumping into and over barrels, climbing a rope on to the roof of a building, jumping from the fourth floor, and finally hanging on to another rope let down from an airplane. The whole of this action proceeds at breakneck speed. The theme of the stolen documents was clearly no more than a pretext for realizing an "urban spectacle" in which the stage decorations, the death-defying feats of the thief and the "cinematographic speed" (*kinematografičeskaja skorost'*) with which they were performed played the leading role.

---

[8] The title *Priemyš* is no doubt given tongue in cheek, considering the stature of the notion *priem* (device) in the Russian *avant-garde* theater. Cf. Arvatov's discussion of how to "proletarianize . . . the devices" (*proletarizirovat' . . . priemy*), *O teatre*, p. 115.

The Popular Comedy's second period, from the winter season 1920–21 to the dissolution of the group in January, 1922, signified a sort of reaction in terms of repertoire and a reversion to earlier restorationist tendencies. Plays by Shakespeare, Molière and Calderon were performed and the Popular Comedy came to resemble the Ancient Theater (*Starinnyj teatr*) with an orchestra on stage playing antique instruments. The circus arena was exchanged for the earlier platform stage that was now conceived of as the reconstructed Shakespearean stage.

In connection with his production of Shakespeare's *The Merry Wives of Windsor* Radlov wrote that "in order for the comedy to become popular, it has to base itself on earlier centuries' popular theater . . ." complemented by "the style and character of our times" (*Istorija sovetskogo teatra* p. 203). Radlov tried to explain what these characteristics were in a passage that could have come straight out of Marinetti's *Variety Theater Manifesto*: "A swiftness which only we possess; types distinguished by their grotesque exaggeration; eccentricism as the new form of world view created by the Anglo-American genius—all this has to begin to shine through in the budding 20th century popular comedy" (ibid.).[9]

With these considerations in mind the Popular Comedy plunged into the classical repertoire in search of a style and character to reflect the theater's "modernist-urbanist" ambitions. Shakespeare's play was presented from the standpoint of its temporal and spatial peculiarities, and in an effort to determine the principles of a truly Shakespearean approach, Radlov and his collegues tried to wring mathematical formulations from the structure of the play. The intention was to convey "the charming flow of the action, its constant fluctuation" (ibid. p. 204) and to emphasize how Shakespeare would move his characters from one part of the stage to another in increasingly varied patterns. The level of abstraction in these experiments continued to rise. In a performance directed by Solov'ev in the Italian improvised comedy tradition the stress lay on "the clarity of the gesture and the swiftness of the dialogue" (ibid.). Another play in the same tradition and with the same director resulted in little more

[9] Cf. Marinetti 1972 p. 121.

than a catalogue of different techniques and devices used in the farce. At this point critical voices began to be heard even among the theater's most devout friends who were wondering what in these exercises made them qualify for the label "popular". As an ultimate result of this mounting criticism the Popular Comedy dissolved in January, 1922.

7.

The "futurization" of the Russian theater, implying the introduction of popular forms of entertainment (the circus in particular) and the focus on abstract features of space, time and motion in the plays, resulted in a strong tendency toward complete disintegration of the dramatic and thematic coherence of the performance. This result was already noted at that time by the critics Konstantin Deržavin and Viktor Šklovskij. Deržavin wrote:

> The circus startles us with its separate elements—through the tiny details in its dangerous or comic stunts. The theater fears above all every partition, every deviation from the unity of action. In Radlov's experiments we sometimes observe a desire to unite these art forms, we see an attempt to find a third unit: an unknown "theater-circus" (*teatro-cirk*) (Zolotnickij 1976 p. 245).

Radlov's Popular Comedy was quickly succeeded by a new and even more death-defying group, The Factory of the Eccentric Actor, called FĖKS. In September, 1922, this group produced an exceedingly "electrified" version of Gogol's *The Marriage* with the participation of former faithful Popular Comedy actors and circus artists. Radlov commented bitterly after the performance that his patent had been stolen by FĖKS Inc. (ibid. p. 264). This particular performance, by the way, is supposed to have been the origin of the satirical account of a certain "Teatr Kolumba" in Il'f and Petrov's *The Twelve Chairs* (Kleberg 1977 p. 101). This source of inspiration becomes quite understandable if we listen to one of the directors in the FĖKS group, Grigorij Kozincev's description of this performance many years later:

> So we tried to [stage] *The Marriage*. I say tried because the thing had no relation either to Gogol''s play or to what one

normally understands by *mise en scène*. The structure of the spectacle, an amalgam of circus, cabaret and cinema, was improvised and immediately modified as having already become old hat. We were haunted by all sorts of vague notions which were immediately supplanted by others, still more fantastic, still more imprecise . . .

And he contines:

We were only allowed to get on to the stage on the day of the première, and for only two hours before curtain rise. We were still rehearsing with the actors while the audience was kicking up a great din in the foyer, demanding that the doors be opened and the show begin. During this time, straddled across the proscenium barrier, a young man with a huge forehead and a lot of hair was hurrying us, dominating the other noise. 'Too slow!' he was shouting in a sharp voice; and again 'Much too slow! Speed up the action!'. It was Sergej Eisenstein. I must add one remark; we might be accused of all sorts of faults, but slowness was not one of them! . . . (*Cinema in Revolution* p. 101).

Kozincev was probably right, slowness was not the main problem of Annenkov's, Radlov's and the FEKS group's efforts to create a genuinely popular form of theater. Viktor Šklovskij may have come closer to the heart of the matter than Ėjzenštejn when he pointed out that Annenkov's and Radlov's theater existed outside the word or that the word was on the decline in their theater. This tendency represented a sharp break with the popular arts because, as he put it, "the popular theater, the Russian in particular, is not simply a theater of movement in general, but a theater of verbal dynamism" (Šklovskij 1923 pp. 136–137). From that perspective it would come as no surprise that the eccentric theater gravitated toward the non-verbal art of space, time and dynamism, the art of the electric age: the silent cinema.[10]

[10] Cf. Selezneva: "The future theater is a theater of psychology and the word. The film is not accessible to either of them. The specific character of the film is movement and silence" (Selezneva 1972 p. 10).

In the early summer of 1922 Radlov expressed a desire to make a film based on his play *The Foster-Child*. There was a certain logic in his wish, considering the theme and action of the play, but Radlov never received the opportunity. However Kozincev and Trauberg of the FÉKS group produced *The Adventures of Oktjabrina* in 1924, the same year Lev Kulešov made *The Strange Adventures of Mr. West in the Land of the Bolsheviks*. Both films had many thriller and action features in common with *The Foster-Child*.

In 1922 Radlov also wrote a curious, in part almost ecstatic, article called "The Electrification of the Theater". The article once again raised the issue of the director's dictatorial "single will" and ability to turn the performance into a synthesis of the arts. The discussion about how the director could integrate all theatrical elements, the actors included, into an orchestra-like unity had preoccupied the Symbolists at the beginning of the century. Their use of musical analogies and terms were followed by Radlov when he attempted a Futurist solution to the problem. "Since every *culture* carries its particular sense of time and space", he declared, "the theater will reflect it in a more encompassing and sharper way than the other arts" (Radlov 1929 p. 93). He maintained, echoing Marinetti, that we live in a world of electricity and we must therefore carry the electrification of the theater to its logical conclusion. Radlov seems to have had something close to a religious experience in the summer of 1920, when he co-directed a mass spectacle in Petrograd guiding the masses with some sort of electric conductor's baton:[11] "What perfect bliss— to feel, carry, watch over stage time! To be the master of the theatrical minutes! To wave the conductor's baton!" (ibid. p. 99).

Some directors had tried to revolutionize the theater by dragging the masses on stage, fully equipped with rifles, horses and trucks, creating obvious spatial problems. Radlov instead sought to bring them under artistic control in the squares of Petrograd waving a conductor's baton. Sergej Éjzenštejn, who realized the limitation of both these approaches, left the theater altogether for the film, which promised greater freedom and possibilities in the artistic treatment of

[11] This mass spectacle took place on July 19th in the honor of the Second Comintern Congress and was called "Long Live the World Commune!" ("K mirovoj kommune").

themes involving the masses' actions and movements. One may wonder if Radlov would not have done the same, had he understood the implications of his call for the electrification of the theater. Radlov envisioned his omnipotent director-conductor,[12] the tsar of the theater as he called him, sitting somewhere in the back of the auditorium controlling the events on stage by letting his fingers dance over a complex keyboard. Such artistic control would have had greater prospects of being realized in the emerging cinema of montage[13], which turned out to provide a more encompassing and sharper way of reflecting the electric and revolutionary era's sense of time and space.

Stockholm

---

[12] "The performance is conducted by the author" was the text Radlov suggested for the posters announcing his future electrified productions (Radlov 1929 p. 10).

[13] In fact, Selezneva credits Radlov with the invention of the concept of "associative montage" (*associativnyj montaž*) in film. Cf. Selezneva 1972 p. 20.

References

Arvatov, B.
1922 "Teatr, kak proizvodstvo" *O teatre,* Tver'

Bablet, D.
1966 *Edward Gordon Craig.* London.
Cinema in Revolution, New York 1973.

Hildebrand, O.
1978 *Harlekin Frälsaren.* Teater och verklighet i Nikolaj Evreinovs
dramatik, Uppsala.

Istorija sovetskogo teatra, Leningrad 1933.

Kirby, M.
1971 *Futurist Performance,* New York.

Kleberg, L.
1977 *Teatern som handling.* Sovjetisk avantgardeestetik, 1917–1927.
Stockholm.

Manifesty ital'janskogo futurizma, Moskva 1914.

Marinetti, F.
Selected Writings, New York 1972.

Mejerchol'd, V. È.
1968 *Stat'i, pis'ma, reči, besedy,* 1–2, Moskva.

Meyerhold, V.
1969 *On Theater,* New York.

Radlov, S.
1929 *10 let v teatre,* Leningrad.

Selezneva, T.
1972 *Kinomysl' 1920-ch godov,* Leningrad.

Šklovskij, V.
1923 *Chod konja,* Moskva/Berlin.

Sovetskij teatr. Dokumenty i materialy. 1917–1967, Leningrad 1968.

Zolotnickij, D.
1976 *Zori teatral'nogo oktjabrja,* Leningrad.

Nils Åke Nilsson

Mandel'štam and the Moscow Art Theater

It has been said of Mandel'štam's prose as well as of his poetry that it presents "the life of the epoch in living and plastic images, with all its aptly observed and well chosen, characteristic details" (Filippov p. XXXVIII). It is thus easy to understand that a poet who wrote poems on such topical manifestations of modern life as tennis, the telephone and cinema, football and the American bar (using the names as titles of the poems) should follow with interest and have something to add to the vivid discussions of the 20s on the new experiments in the Russian theater.

Among Mandel'štam's many essays and sketches there are a few published between 1923–27 which discuss contemporary theater. Although usually neglected by Mandel'štam scholars (Przybylski 1966 being an exception) they are worth reading for at least two reasons. They add small but interesting pieces of information to our knowledge of Russian theatrical life of the 20s, while at the same time they are closely connected with Mandel'štam's poetry and esthetic thinking of this period.

One of them, "The Art Theater and the Word" ("Chudožestvennyj teatr i slovo"), was published in the journal *Teatr i muzyka,* 1923, No. 36. Earlier the same year Mandel'štam had printed a short review of Ernst Toller's play *Masse-Mensch*, in the same journal (No. 1–2). Toller was at that time a topical name, although this play had not yet been performed on the Russian stage. The Moscow Art Theater, on the other hand, represented, as it seemed, the very opposite of Toller's revolutionary and collectivistic ideas. While his play was, as Mandel'štam put it, "a play with a future", the Art Theater represented a formula which in this particular political situation seemed to belong entirely to the past. Why then choose to write on this theater?

There is one obvious reason. When Mandel'štam wrote his essay the main troupe of the Art Theater was abroad on a tour which lasted two years, from September 1922 to August 1924. During the civil war, part of the ensemble, including Ol'ga Knipper-Čechova and Kačalov, was trapped in the south of Russia, unable to return to Moscow. When the entire ensemble was reunited three years later, the rather chaotic state of cultural life demanded that some of the theater's famous principles be reconsidered. "We found ourselves in a blind impasse", Stanislavskij later wrote in his *My Life in Art.* "It was necessary to take a look at the whole picture from a distance in order to see how things really were" (Stanislavskij p. 452).

In other words, when Mandel'štam published his article the Art Theater was a topical subject after all, worth commenting on. It seemed clear that one period of its activity had come to an end. Did it still have a future? Or was its time irrevocably gone? Mandel'štam's essay could, in fact, be read as a kind of obituary, a nostalgic backward glance and a critical summary of its significance for the Russian intelligentsia at the turn of the century: "Since the days of my childhood I remember the devotional atmosphere that surrounded this theater. For the intelligentsia to go to the 'Chudožestvennyj' was almost equal to taking communion, to going to church".

Such an approach links the essay with *The Noise of Time,* the prose book published a few years later. The picture of the Art Theater corresponds to what is said here about another contemporary theater dear to the Russian intelligentsia, namely the Komissarževskaja theater in Petersburg: "The truth of the matter is that the Komissarževskaja theater expressed the Protestant spirit of the Russian intelligentsia, the peculiar Protestant spirit of its views on art and the theater".

The juxtaposition of theater and cult was, of course, a typical feature of the period. The special twist here was the "Protestant" frame, the demand for the simplest possible atmosphere—"clean as on a yacht and bare as in a Lutheran church".

Such a decor amounted first of all to a protest—which we recognize from other European theaters at this time—against the fashionable atmosphere of the usual Petersburg and Moscow theaters, against auditoriums in red plush and imperial gold, casts based on a few divas, a particular style of acting. Čechov's reaction to Sara Bernhardt during her performances in Petersburg in 1881 is characteristic of this call for simplicity, and it affords us a certain insight into the background of the emergence of the Moscow Art Theater. Yes, she was probably a great actress and there were moments when one was moved almost to tears. But the tears never materialized because of one thing: the artificial quality of her acting. "Sara Bernhardt's every sigh, her tears, her convulsions in the presence of death, her whole style of acting was nothing but a thoroughly learned and faultlessly presented lesson" (Čechov p. 487).

The "Protestant spirit" further included a repudiation of the popular mysticism connected with Ortodox or Slavophil thinking. Tolstoj's ascetic ideals, the moral austerity of Ibsen, Strindberg's boldness in showing "the whole man", was at that moment more needed than Dostoevskij's ideas or symbolist metaphysics (cf. Andrej Belyj's article "Ibsen and Dostoevskij" 1905, Komissarževskaja's predilection for Ibsen's plays, Blok's "Strindberg years").

Mandel'štam makes yet another point here. This call for a "Protestant spirit" in the theater could also be explained by the simple fact that the intelligentsia never took any real interest in the theater as such. Cultural life focused on literature, on books ("Eto bylo tipično literaturnoe, daže literatorskoe pokolenie"). And so the intelligentsia regarded the theater exclusively as an interpreter of literature, a translator who transposed literary works into another language that was easier to understand. The simplest possible theater buildings, decor, staging and acting were the background against which the literary qualities of the text could best be brought out. Mandel'štam found a Biblical image for this program: the Art Theater, he said, "originated out of a peculiar attempt to touch literature as if it were a living body, to feel it and put one's fingers on it. The pathos of this generation—to which the Art Theater also belonged— was the pathos of a Doubting Thomas". To be sure, Mandel'štam adds, Čechov was a playwright with different ideas, but the sceptical Russian intellectual rooted in Russian realism did not trust him either. Here as well he wanted to "touch" him to be convinced of his reality, as it were.

What Mandel'štam was hinting at here was obviously such things as Čechov's annoyance with Stanislavskij's too realistic approach to his play ("One thing I can say: Stanislavskij has ruined my play", i.e. *The Cherry Orchard*), Stanislavskij's well known predilection for concrete details (singing frogs, whistling trains, genuine birch-trees, the pot-bellied chest of drawers in *The Cherry Orchard*) and for filling dialogues which he found static with speechless acting in the background, these devices which Brjusov later characterized as "unnecessary truth" ("nenužnaja pravda", *Mir iskusstva* 1902:4). Čechov, in other words, was at first performed according to a realistic formula which had been worked out for Ibsen's *An Enemy of the People* and had functioned there with considerable succes. The Čechovian "*nastroenie*" ("mood") was mainly suggested by external means—"all the work of the Art Theater went under the banner of a distrust in the word", is Mandel'štam's conclusion, and it is thus clear—although he does not say so—that he is speaking of the first, naturalistic period of the theater.

In spite of its many innovations, compared with the regular theaters of its time, the Art Theater, as Mandel'štam saw it, never created a real theater in the proper sense of the word, but merely a vehicle for the literary and political ambitions of the Russian intelligentsia. Was such a conclusion just a historical judgement or did his words, in 1923, have a more topical reference? Was he, for instance, suggesting, that now, after the revolution, something new had happened, that perhaps a real theater and a real repertory had appeared?

The beginning of his review of Toller's *Masse-Mensch* seems to point in this direction: he starts by saying that Toller's play is a play "with a future". But it is soon evident that what appeals to him is above all its general structure, even though it is in no way original. It is a play of the same type as Leonid Andreev's *Life of Man*: strong, elementary, easy to understand thanks to a simple plot and straightforward symbolism. This plot is very topical, treating of the collision between the best heritage of the old world, its humanism, and "the new collective imperative, '*Tat*'". Perhaps is it this theme which justifies the somewhat ambiguous opinion: "a play with a future". The tragedy of the female protagonist, Mandel'štam says, is the tragedy of Toller himself, "who overcame and outgrew his humanism in the name of action". We, of course, recognize this theme from Mandel'štam's poetry, where in the collision between the old world and the new one of the 20s he definitely sides with the humanistic heritage.

The critical points he makes here, however, are more interesting, since they clearly accord with his criticism of the Art Theater. Toller, he says, belongs to a group calling itself "Dramatische Wille". The name is misleading, since "this 'will' actually lies outside the realm of the theater". His strong and noble instinct "splashes across the theater, cleanses it; it does not create anything for the theater as such, however, but merely acts through it, using it only as a vehicle". Toller, as the title of the essay says, is not a revolutionary playwright but a revolutionary in the theater, i.e. a revolutionary who adopts the theater to his political purposes. The result is a schematism of plot which seems to be typical of all European revolutionary plays. The revolution and the masses are presented in the form of a political rally—"ėto splošnoj miting". This is naive, improbable and very unconvincing, since "the important events that determine the course of a revolution are never born at a political rally". This is a view which certainly did not correspond to Lenin's ideas, but rather echoes the "stichijnyj" interpretation of the revolution popular among the Socialist-Revolutionaries and many writers in the early 1920s.

As Mandel'štam saw it there existed a clear correspondence between the Moscow Art Theater of the 1890s and the revolutionary theater of the 1920s. In both cases the theater functioned above all as a vehicle for certain political or cultural ideas. A distrust of "the word" is linked with a need to "touch" the text, to explain it and interpret it for certain specific purposes. Already in the essay "The Word and Culture" from 1921 the image of Doubting Thomas appears with a direct reference to the revolutionary demands: "Do not", Mandel'štam turns to the critics of the period, "demand from poetry any special substantiality, materiality, or concreteness. It is the very same revolutionary hunger. The Doubt of Thomas. Why is you must touch it with your finger?"

What kind of theater then did Mandel'štam advocate? A central point here is, as in his poetry from this period, the concept of "slovo". This word appears in the title of several articles, besides that on the Art Theater also two of his main essays on poetry in the early 20s, "The Word and Culture" ("Slovo i kul'tura", 1921) and "On the Nature of the Word" ("O prirode slova", 1922).

The latter essay speaks of a "Russian Nominalism", a conception of the reality of the word itself "which refreshes the spirit of our language". The future belongs—after the romantic, symbolist, futurist and imaginist attempts to adopt language to their needs—to a "living poetry of word-subjects". The well-known lines from 1920— "for the blessed senseless word/ I will pray in the Soviet night" ("*za blažennoe bessmyslennoe slovo* / *Ja v sovetskoj noči pomoljus'*")— refers apparently to such word-objects which could protect the poet and Russian poetry like magic spells or talismans (on Mandel'štam's talismanic imagery, see Ronen p. 151 f.). "Meaningless" could here, as Broyde suggests (Broyde p. 28), be translated as "aimless". This links the line with other statements of this period directed against the official utilitarian view on art ("poor poetry shies away from the countless revolver muzzles of the unconditional demands aimed at it. What should poetry be? Perhaps it is not obliged to be anything; perhaps it has no obligation to anyone; perhaps its creditors are all fraudulent", "The Thrust", 1924).

Russian nominalism is, as Mandel'štam sees it, opposite to a European trend which transforms words into clear-cut and useful terms, i.e. not into living but dead objects. This is why in "The Word and Culture" he asked "why equate the word with the thing, with grass, with the object it designates?" The thing, Mandel'štam stressed in this often quoted statement, is not the master of the word. "The living word"—and one should note the modifier here—does not designate an object "but freely chooses for its dwelling place" this or that "beloved body", wanders freely around the thing "like the soul around an abandoned, but not forgotten body".

How would such a program work in the theater? It is obvious that Mandel'štam does not accept Stanislavskij's mimetic system and it is equally clear that he repudiates Mejerchol'd's conventional program (cf. his review of a Kiev theater from 1925: "The Ukrainian actors gasp for breath like poisoned mice in those Tolleresque and Kaiseresque cages as well as in the Sinclair play which is garnished à la Toller" ("Berezil"). Mandel'štam evidently looked for a third alternative, focusing on "a ressurection of the word" in the theater.

His articles on poetry and the theater of this time were a general defense of the ambiguity and polyvalence of poetic language against "the revolver muzzles of strict demand aimed at it". They opposed the transformation of the "living" language into political slogans, utilitarian terms and practical abbreviations, i.e. into "dead terms", following the western trend (cf. the vivid discussion at this time around "Russian" and "Soviet", "literary and vulgar", "classical" and "proletarian" language).

It was not only an attempt to emphasize the text itself against the dominance of the stage directors and against the wild theatrical experiments of the time. It advocated more specifically a handling of the text which would bring into focus the "word-objects" and their connotations, the word's looking for "a beloved body", the very procedure of such a wandering and searching—which included also the very sound and ring of the "meaningless" word. Here was a clear connection with "transrational" poetry (cf. the "zaumnyj son" in his "hayloft poem", see Taranovski p. 21–23).

An interesting parallel is offered by a pamphlet called *The Phonetics of Theater* (*Fonetika teatra*), published by Aleksej Kručenych the same year, 1923, when Mandel'štam printed his article on the Moscow Art Theater. It was an attempt to adjust the futurist *zaum'*, "transrational language", to the new political and social situation. "*Zaum'* was no longer a formalistic device but a social dialect", Boris Kušner maintained in the preface. Since a time of revolution is a time of strong emotions and swift dynamism, transrational language, in Kručenych's opinion, could better express the feelings of the time than ordinary speech. It had the same condensed structure as the film, and for that reason it would be an excellent "emotional accompaniment" to films; special theaters should be built for the purpose. And when the film some day begins to talk, its language will certainly be *zaum'*!

But transrational language was also of importance to the modern theater for at least two reasons. It was, to begin with, "throat hygiene". No less than our eyes, our ears and throats need new materials to work with. Transrational language could renew the theater, because "if an actor cannot convince the audience by merely phonetic means (sound, intonation, rhythm) no 'meaning' will help him". For the sake of oral training the theater should stage "transrational plays" (or, at least, use the examples given in the pamphlet as a kind of daily exercise). Furthermore, transrational language is also "linguistic hygiene". It renews and refreshes ordinary speech, bringing out its phonetic and metaphorical treasures. It is an international language and thus the poetic language of the future!

Mandel'štam would hardly have agreed that transrational plays could solve the problem of "distrust in the word", but he might have endorsed the statement that the voice of an actor is more important than the conventional meaning of the text. His most favorable theater review, "Jachontov", as a matter of fact, deals with the one-man theater of Vladimir Jachontov, who between 1927 and 1935 toured the Soviet Union with a repertory of text montages and a minimum of stage props. The remarkable thing about this young actor, Mandel'štam writes, was not only that he was able to fill the whole stage with his acting but above all the fact he, "uniquely among contemporary Russian actors, moves in the word, as in a space". He is, as Mandel'štam puts it, not just an actor who reads and interprets a text but a genuine reader who, being on the same level as the author, discusses and argues with him.

He similarly described another of his favorite actors of the 20s, Michoels, director of the Jewish chamber theater. He was also able to fill the stage with his acting and lend theater props or objects from daily life an aura of historical and existential significance. When in one of his plays he walks down the street "the audience can actually hear the snow crunching under the felt boots issued to him by the Education Commission. Such an actor must be kept off the realistic stage—things will just melt away under his touch. He creates his own props—a needle and thread, a glass of pepper vodka, a mirror, any object from daily life that he needs—whenever he takes it into his head to do so". And when he merely utters the words: Narkompros! Narkompros! they resound "like deep sighs from an aeolian harp" and communicate better to the audience than any long monologue "the fever of a historical day".

These characterizations should be compared with the chapter on Komissarževskaja in *The Noise of Time*. "The theater has lived and will live by the human voice", Mandel'štam emphasizes here. Komissarževskaja was one of the few to understand this truth: "Unlike the Russian actors of that day—and also, perhaps, of the present day— Komissarževskaja possessed an inner sense of music; she raised and lowered her voice just as the breathing of the verbal sentence required. Her acting was three-quarters verbal and was accompanied only by the most essential, economical gestures".

The opposite of this kind of acting is what Mandel'štam called "the pig snout of declamation". He finds it not only in the imperial theatres but in the Art Theater as well, especially among its actresses. By "declamation" Mandel'štam apparently had in mind an intonation which imposed itself on the text and did not correspond to the natural rhythm of the phrase. Instead of letting the phrase unfold itself freely, a "doubting Thomas" tried to adjust it to a certain purpose or scheme. Komissarževskaja's voice apparently had this freedom which did not limit "the word"; understanding and respecting its nature as a "Psyche", she opened it up to a multitude of meanings.

What Mandel'štam was looking for in modern Russian theater was a resurrection of such a freedom of the word. There were only short glimpses to be had of it. His dream of a "theater of the word" was destined never to materialize.

References

H. Broyde, *Osip Mandel'štam and his Age*, Cambridge, Mass. 1975.
A. P. Čechov, *Polnoe sobranie sočinenij*, t. I, Moskva 1944.
B. Fillippov, "Proza Mandel'štama", *Sobranie sočinenij v dvuch tomach*, t. II, Washington 1966.
O. Mandelsztam, "Artykuły o teatrze", przełożył Ryszard Przybylski, *Dialog* 1966, nr 10.
O. Ronen, "An introduction to Mandel'štam's Slate Ode and 1. January 1924. Similarity and Complementarity", *Slavica Hierosolymitana*, vol. IV, 1979.
K. Stanislavskij, *My Life in Art*, Moscow n.d.
K. Taranovski, *Essays on Mandel'štam*, Cambridge, Mass., 1976.

The English quotations from "The Art Theater and the Word", "A Revolutionary in the Theater", "The Thrust", "Jachontov", "Michoels" and "Berezil" are from Osip Mandel'štam, *The Complete Critical Prose and Letters*. Ed. by J. G. Harris, Ann Arbor 1979; certain inadequacies have been corrected. *The Noise of Time* is quoted from *The Prose of Osip Mandel'štam*. Translated by Clarence Brown, Princetown 1965.